SALES PERSPECTIVE

SHIFT YOUR MINDSET
IGNITE YOUR SALES POTENTIAL
STAND OUT FROM THE CROWD

"If you are looking to ignite your sales potential, this book is for you. Jimmy Z brings a fresh approach to the world of sales with a proven method that will turn your strategy into high-impact results. A simple shift in your Sales Perspective allows you to set aside traditional closing tactics, make amazing connections, and deliver what matters most to your customers. You'll learn to stop closing and start connecting to add value to your customers and stand out from the crowd."

—**Dr. Kary Oberbrunner,** *Wall Street Journal* **and** *USA Today* **bestselling author of 14 books, CEO of Igniting Souls and Blockchain Life, and Berry Chair of Entrepreneurship at Cedarville University.**

"The secret to effective communication starts with focusing on the relationship. I have experienced first-hand how Jimmy Z brings his desire to add value to others through his ability to make great connections. Let SALES PERSPECTIVE be your new resource for shifting your focus from the transaction to the relationship and ignite your selling potential to build lasting relationships. If you are looking to crack the code to genuinely connect with your prospects through an authentic conversation and earn the opportunity to serve them, this book is for you."

—**Rick Larson, co-founder of Larson Educational Services and PROSOURCE Educational Services. Inspiring speaker, trainer, teacher, and coach.**

"SALES PERSPECTIVE, will guide you in turning your approach to transactions into great experiences! Jimmy Z brings a passion to add value to the customer in ways that separate him from others in his field. His fresh approach to the sales process leads you in focusing on the connection and relationship with your prospect or customer, on what *they* want—their desires, needs, and aspirations—rather than on what you want. The path to success lies in growing your business by serving others."

—**B. Joseph Pine II, author of** *The Experience Economy*, *Authenticity*, *Infinite Possibility*, **and** *Mass Customization* **as well as an internationally acclaimed author, speaker, and management advisor to Fortune 500 companies and entrepreneurial start-ups alike.**

"The sales process has always been more about connections than transactions. In this book you will discover the road map to making better connections and delivering lasting value to your customers. Jimmy Z has consistently brought the value of connection to my business, and I highly recommend this book if you want to stand out from the crowd in your sales pursuits."

—**Dustin Swenson, Vice President of Sales, Nesbit Agencies.**

"The world of sales is truly a people business. Jimmy Z exemplifies this approach consistently and is all about serving the customer. Jimmy's curious nature has always served him well and delivering value to others is paramount to the way he goes about connecting with prospects, clients, and customers. This book is filled with stories that show the importance of putting the customer's needs first in every conversation. I highly recommend this valuable resource. Your business will grow as a result of putting SALES PERSPECTIVE into practice every day."

—**Terry Didion, retired Sales Director for Meadowbrook Insurance.**

"Jimmy Z brings his authentic approach to every conversation. As a clear communicator and coach, Jimmy is passionate about adding value to others on a daily basis. This consistent method of connecting allows him to make a difference in the lives of others. Invest your time in learning from this valuable resource to grow your ability to connect with your prospects and customers. SALES PERSPECTIVE contains a proven method that will help you stand out from your competition and make a difference in the lives of those you serve."

—**Troy Noor, President, Boulevard Wealth Management.**

"It has been my experience that Jimmy Z lives what he shares in this book! His strategy has helped me refine my approach and his ability to build relationships is one of his greatest strengths. If you are looking for a clear and concise method for turning your prospects into lifelong customers, this book is for you!"

—Eric Klein, Senior VP, Assured Partners of Minnesota.

"Making quality connections with people has always been a strong suit of Jimmy's approach to life. If you are looking for a road map to consistently add value to others, I encourage you to consider digging into SALES PERSPECTIVE. Here you will learn to pursue the most important perspective in sales, and quite frankly, in life—serving the needs of others. Let Jimmy Z lead you to climb to new heights and make a difference in the lives of others."

—Brigadier General, Charles Causey, is a U.S. Army Chaplain, and author of several books, including *Candor, Unbreakable,* and *Words and Deeds: Becoming a Man of Courageous Integrity.*

SALES PERSPECTIVE

SHIFT YOUR MINDSET
IGNITE YOUR SALES POTENTIAL
STAND OUT FROM THE CROWD

JIMMY ZUGSCHWERT

SALES PERSPECTIVE © 2024 by Jimmy Zugschwert. All rights reserved.

Published by Author Academy Elite
PO Box 43, Powell, OH 43065
AuthorAcademyElite.com

All rights reserved. No part of this publication may be reproduced, distributed, or transmitted in any form or by any means, including photocopying, recording, or other electronic or mechanical methods, without the prior written permission of the publisher, except in the case of brief quotations embodied in critical reviews and certain other noncommercial uses permitted by copyright law.

LCCN: 2024917004
ISBN: 979-8-88583-367-7 (paperback)
ISBN: 979-8-88583-368-4 (hardback)
ISBN: 979-8-88583-369-1 (e-book)

Available in paperback, hardback, e-book, and audiobook.

Any Internet addresses (websites, blogs, etc.) and telephone numbers printed in this book are offered as a resource. They are not intended in any way to be or imply an endorsement by Author Academy Elite, nor does Author Academy Elite vouch for the content of these sites and numbers for the life of this book.

Some names and identifying details have been changed to protect the privacy of individuals.

To my amazing wife, Nancy:
Your love and support over the years have inspired my self-confidence and helped me grow in ways that allowed me to add value to others throughout my sales journey.

To my personal Board of Directors:
Dave, John, Andy, Joe, and Ken: Thank you. Your wisdom, insight, and experience have encouraged me to climb higher personally and professionally.

CONTENTS

How to Get the Most from this Book — 1
A Note to You—the Reader

Introduction — 9

PART ONE: THE DISCONNECT

New Perspective (Definition)

Chapter 1: Sales Perspective — 17
First Things First

New Strategy (Sales Perspective)

Chapter 2: The Perspective Mindset — 39
Redefining WIN-WIN

Chapter 3: Close the Gap — 51
Overcoming the Disconnect, Eliminate Assumptions, and Get to the Heart of the Matter

Chapter 4: Stop Trying to Close the Sale — 73
Let Curiosity Lead You — Uncover What They Want and Give Them Access to It

PART TWO: THE BRIDGE

The Framework (Goals)

Chapter 5: The Essential Selling Perspective (ESP) Method — 91
Featuring the FIVE Cs of Every Sales Experience — Your New Game Plan for Success

The Process (System)

Chapter 6: **CARE**	113
Preparation Makes All the Difference	
Chapter 7: **CONNECT**	125
Rapport — Build a Bridge of Influence	
Chapter 8: **CLARIFY**	141
Value Proposition — Simplify Your Message	
Chapter 9: **CONFIRM**	161
Accuracy — Review and Acknowledge Unity	
Chapter 10: **COMMIT**	173
Specific Next Steps — Agreed Upon Outcome	
Chapter 11: Finish Well	183
Handling Objections — Follow Up and Follow Through	

PART THREE: YOUR NEW WORLD

The Future (New Road Map)

Chapter 12: How to Be Welcome Anywhere	199
Be part of the Solution	

Chapter 13: Build Lasting Relationships — 211
People Matter Most

Chapter 14: The BIG Picture — 223
Your Sales Legacy

APPENDIX

The Sales Perspecitve Game Plan	239
The Sales Perspective Reading Plan	243
About the Author	245
Endnotes	251

How to Get the Most From This Book

A NOTE TO YOU — THE READER

What started out as a simple idea has become a passionate pursuit. Early in my sales career, I found that I got more joy in my work when I made a connection with my customer and added value to their lives beyond the transaction. This was a departure from the standard sales tactics and strategies that were pervasive in the market. Owners and managers measured sales results by looking at data. Most measures were built around the number of deals closed, products sold, inventory moved, quotas met, bonuses earned, and bottom-line results. The sales metrics were always looming and top-of-mind with management. Numbers and reports were their story-line. They could barely see any other factors that held significance when measuring sales success.

As I spent time in the marketplace, it became evident to me that the sales process was so much more than the transaction. I found the importance of adding value to my prospects and customers was an integral part of the *entire* sale. You will discover in this book the bigger picture of sales wrapped in a framework and process that provides a proven method of engaging your clients, customers, and prospects. Together, we will uncover the keys to each of the sales components including the preparation, pre-sale, connection, discovery, engagement, confirmation, follow-up, follow-through, post-sale, and purpose.

AN INTRIGUING IDEA. When my sales career expanded to a larger territory, I was introduced to the idea that I was the CEO of my territory. This meant that I was responsible for accomplishing my sales goals (quotas and growth) in the best ways possible. It was also permission for me to personalize the process. With this newfound freedom and direction, I knew that if I could find a duplicatable way to govern my time, energy, and effort, I would be on my way to unlocking my potential by putting my strengths to work in adding value to my prospects and customers. This strategy allowed me to think beyond my numbers and start caring about *who* I was serving. Once I made this shift, my numbers started to take care of themselves. As a result of my strategy to connect with others and serve their needs, I was now consistently hitting my goals.

Focus is an amazing thing. When you are focused on closing the sale, your mindset, strategy, questions, thoughts, directives, needs, and pressure are all driven by your perspective. Being in the game of closing the deal often means being on the attack.

"Don't let them off the hook."

"The sale isn't complete until they sign on the dotted line."

"Put the ball in their court and keep it there until they agree to buy."

"Always Be Closing."

"They need this deal, because I need this deal."

"Don't take 'No' for an answer."

"A 'No' is just a reason to keep on selling them."

This can get exhausting and so self-focused that you'll rarely win a relationship that can lead to repeat sales or referrals. I've learned that people don't like to be sold, they like to buy.

Hold on. Do you mean I should pay attention to what my prospect thinks? If it's true that their perspective matters, why would I ever back them into a corner to get them to say 'yes' without ever getting to know what they want?

Hello!

ADDING VALUE. When I embraced the idea of adding value to my prospects and customers, my perspective changed. This led me on a journey of making genuine connections to uncover what *they* were really looking for. As I put the needs of my customer first, my eyes were opened to a world of authentic relationships that brought me a sense of joy the transaction could never fulfill. I was building bridges and delivering value. This one change in my strategy became a framework for becoming welcome anywhere. People knew that I was there for them and not for myself. It helped me redefine WIN-WIN and set me on the road to winning without any pressure to close the deal.

People like to do business with people they like. This doesn't mean being likable is your only strategy, but it is an important ingredient to building a bridge with others.

There are times in your personal and professional development, where the most strategic approach you can take is to keep it simple. This is your opportunity to do just that—take the simple approach. Getting started right begins with your mindset. This is where your willingness to think differently becomes your advantage.

BE THE BEST YOU. I have always taken the mental posture that I am in charge of the things I can control. After all, I am the CEO of my territory. In his book *The E Mind*, author Kary Oberbrunner, helps us grasp the importance of our mindset in striving for growth and success. "Today's economy and marketplace require every single person to think like an entrepreneur. Those who do will succeed. Those who refuse will not. It's that simple." [1]

When striving toward excellence and success in business and in life, keep in mind that there are things you can control and things out of your control. Make sure to keep your focus on things you can control and don't be overly concerned about what's outside of your control. This will free you to focus on being the best you. When your mindset is right, your focus in the sales world leads you to build the best relationships with your prospects and customers.

WRITE YOUR OWN NARRATIVE. In sales, there are often scripts, patterns, talking points, or methods to follow. These are designed to help you with understanding and communicating the value proposition offered by your company. There are important elements and company specific advantages that are vital for you to know as you communicate with prospects and customers. One of the greatest mistakes that many young sales professionals fall into is memorizing or reading the script verbatim. In an effort to make sure they cover everything, their focus is so wrapped up in the scripted narrative that they sound mechanical. This can be a quick turn-off to a prospect. They don't want to be thought of as a number or simply the next name on your call list. Your prospect is a human being. They are busy and don't have time for someone who isn't authentic.

It's time for you to move beyond the script and make the message your own. Personalizing the narrative is one of the most effective ways to gain and keep the attention of your prospects. Your goal should not be to recite the same narrative for every prospect. It should be to create a unique narrative for each prospect by learning about them first. Don't get ahead of yourself and get caught up in what you have to say. As you ask questions of your prospect, use each answer as an opportunity to create their unique narrative. As you gain their attention by striving to learn what's most important to them, they will open up and provide you with the information that will help you discover what they value most. Once you accumulate enough information to determine if your products or services can deliver a solution to their needs, you are on your way to using the correct narrative that they can relate to.

In this book, you will be introduced to a proven methodology that helps you keep your focus on the needs of your prospects and customers. Use these tools as guidelines to organize your thinking and keep your focus on your prospect, and then craft the narrative in your own language. When it feels authentic, your prospect will give you their attention. In a world that is constantly striving to capture your prospect's attention, you have the opportunity to be a difference-maker. Be real. Be genuine. Be authentic. Your credibility will grow, and you may surprise yourself at how your approach will separate you from your competition.

Take your time and embrace the fundamentals. It's also a good habit to review them at least annually and then update your narrative to keep it fresh for your prospects and customers.

SALES PERSPECTIVE HABITS. At the completion of each chapter you'll see a set of specific Sales Perspective Habits to review. You'll find these in a pattern that outlines your winning **S-A-L-E-S** game plan:

Start – take action from right where you are

Analyze – examine your options to begin building your game plan

Learn – spend time getting to know your customer and their business

Engage – reach out and connect to discover common ground

Serve – keep your heart focused on giving to meet the needs of your customers

Start by buildings these habits in your own sales game plan, then pass it on to your team and you will be amazed at how you'll grow as a group and impact others.

YOUR NEXT STEP. At the end of the book, you'll receive instructions on how to take "Your Next Step." Take this invitation to heart. Action is the key to incorporating ideas and principles into your daily habits. Embrace the directive and spend time reviewing the principles you've learned in each chapter. Taking action with what you've learned is a habit that pays consistently over time. Start implementing the principles each day and you'll find yourself building your knowledge and confidence in sales and in life.

SAGE ADVICE. I've been blessed over the years to have many wise people speak into my life. In their own ways, they have all spoken of the importance of focusing on the people you are serving. There is no substitute for adding value to other people. It is one of the most joyous parts of selling goods and services. Plus you will always feel good about yourself for what you do, how you do it, and what you stand for.

Amazing things are ahead for you when you open your heart and mind to a new perspective—the SALES PERSPECTIVE.

All the best,

Jimmy Z

INTRODUCTION

"IT'S NOT COMPLICATED." You may have heard this statement from sales managers or coaches to help you focus on closing as many deals as you can, rather than unravel the complexities you might face in any sales experience. The truth is that sales can be filled with circumstances you can't always anticipate. What you really need to know is how to navigate through the elements of a particular sale when the unexpected occurs.

It may sound counterintuitive, but the main thrust of sales is not the transaction. Now I know, if you are talking to your company's management or ownership, they are looking at the number of transactions monthly, quarterly, or annually. If it's drilled into your mindset to close as many deals as possible, no matter what it takes, you may hit your sales goals or even earn bonuses, but you may also leave a trail of dead bodies—people who you don't really care to know and from whom you won't have the opportunity to get any referrals—because they are nothing more than a transaction to you.

In my early days of selling, my dad, who was also my boss, would tell me, "Son, life's a people business! You have to figure out how to work well and get along with others. If you can do that, you will be successful." Sounds simple, doesn't it? Well, over the years of trying many different sales strategies, I have found the general rule of working well and getting along with others to be golden! But it's not about being liked. As you'll see in chapters 5-10, it starts with the value you provide, the service you deliver, and the trust you build with every customer.

Your perspective needs to be focused on serving—not selling—your clients, customers, and prospects. Throughout this book I will be sharing stories, experiences, outcomes, and lessons learned. I encourage you to pay close attention to what perspectives worked and then make them your own. This isn't a book with a bunch of standard practices and scripts to follow. It is your guide to customize to your unique selling situation. Your authenticity and credibility depend on it. Be genuine. Be the best you, and people will want to do business with you. Shift your perspective to the people side of things and you won't have to worry about your numbers. They will take care of themselves when you provide the value, service, and trust that meet the needs of your customers.

Tough Lesson

"We like doing business with you, but your company's service level is the worst we have ever dealt with, and I can no longer represent that lack of service to our customers. Please cancel my contract." These words cut right through me! I had the privilege of working with this organization for over nine years and had built a solid relationship with the owner and many members of their team. I apologized for my company's failure to live up to our promise and told him I would process his request right away. I thanked him for his business, and even though he told me this was not about me personally, I took little solace in knowing that. After all, I was the one representing my company, even in our failure to deliver value to this agency. It broke my heart that something out of my control irreversibly changed the relationship I had built over the years.

This story is indicative of the failure of an organization to have and maintain the most important perspective in their business. In my sales career, I have worked at times with organizations that have departments operating primarily as silos. In other words, each department stays focused only on their own responsibilities and they don't see the importance of collaboration, coordination, or partnering with other departments to deliver the ultimate value to the customer. This describes the great disconnect when different roles or departments in an organization each hold fast to their own perspective about what's most important.

When an organization loses focus on the big picture, they fail to recognize when different roles or departments are operating from different perspectives. If the company's focus is only on closing deals, they will miss seeing the trail of debris left behind them.

In the sales department, leadership uses numbers as their measure of success, but in the marketplace, sales are driven by relationships. People like to do business with people who help them solve their immediate issues and provide long-term strategies and solutions. This is the main thrust of building partnerships. Don't get me wrong. Sales can and should be measured by numbers, but that's only part of the story. Sales professionals know the importance of building relationships that lead to the long-term partnership that both parties are striving to establish.

Why partnerships? When a partnership doesn't exist and a problem arises, the response from you or your customer can tend to be dismissive. Your boss might tell you to terminate the contract of a client that is not fulfilling their original commitment or your company's expectations. You may be instructed to share this type of dialogue: "I'm sorry this relationship is not working. You haven't met our volume requirements, and you aren't using us enough to merit building a partnership. Why don't we just call it a day? I will proceed to shut down your code and I wish you the best in your future endeavors." Straight forward, right? By the numbers and by the book.

But the sales process is nuanced. When measuring numbers as the only qualifying criteria for success or future potential, one of the most important ingredients is left out of the valuation of the client and their potential. The most important element in the Sales Perspective is relationships.

The term partnership demonstrates the desired commitment on the part of both the company and the client or customer. If you want to build a sustainable business relationship, commit to building partnerships.

My sales career has led me through great successes and great challenges. Notice that I said *led me through*. I chose not to get stuck or completely lose, even in the toughest situations. I built my reputation on developing partnerships where my clients and customers knew that I was for them. They were important to me. I wanted their success. I wanted the best outcome we could attain, even in difficult circumstances. When people sense that you are their partner, they give you their partnership in return. This principle plays out in amazing ways throughout the message, framework, and process found in this book.

My goal for you is that the perspective, ideas, and the game plan shared in these pages will lead you to a greater level of connection and success in your sales journey. Ultimately, your sales success is all in your perspective.

PART ONE
THE DISCONNECT

SALES PERSPECTIVE

FIRST THINGS FIRST

"The greatest tragedy for any human being is going through their entire lives believing the only perspective that matters is their own." [2]

—Doug Baldwin

IN SOME WAYS, IT feels like it was just yesterday. Selling has been such a normal part of my life for so long that when I pause and look back to my early days in business, it doesn't seem that long ago. Do you remember when you started out in your sales career? For some of you, this may have been a while ago and for others it may have started much more recently. I have been in sales for decades, yet I still remember the first time I had the realization that my perspective was off. I missed the mark. Not only did I not make the sale, but I went back to the office with no real clue as to why. Initially, the only thing I could think of was I seemed to be focused only on me and what I had to say. I lacked curiosity. I didn't really know what my prospect was looking for.

I told him everything I knew, and he still did not buy! My enthusiasm seemed to energize only me. It did not have the same effect on my prospect. Yes, I was young, and I prided myself on product knowledge. I believed that I needed to know everything about what I was selling to lift my belief in the benefits my products would deliver to anyone willing to listen. You may be seeing—or even relating to—how young Jimmy was disconnected from the most important perspective in sales: The perspective that takes priority in any sales situation belongs to the customer. Let's look at a couple of examples.

A Common Tale

It's a new day for Joe. He just landed the sales job he had been pursuing for months. After his orientation and company training, he is on his way to his first appointment with a prospective customer. Joe carries all the elements of a new salesperson. He's excited, confident, and of course, a bit nervous. His energy and enthusiasm for the products and services he is selling will help compel him to deliver all the benefits of what he has to offer his prospect.

He is ten minutes early to his appointment and after checking in with the receptionist, he waits in the lobby going through his final checklist to make sure that he has everything with him that he'll need to make the sale.

Sara and Steve Wilson, the sibling owners of Wilson Companies, greet Joe and escort him into a nearby conference room. Joe immediately thanks them for giving him their time so he can share about his company's products and services. Steve says, "We've heard about your company. Tell us more."

Joe begins to share the company history and the development of their products and services over the decades they have been in business in this market.

Sara interrupts Joe to ask a WIIFM (What's In It For Me) question. She asks, "What do you have to offer that can help us?"

Without missing a beat, Joe begins a deep dive into all the benefits for each product and service he represents. (In sales, this is often referred to as a benefits spill – where the salesperson proceeds to share all the features and benefits without any focus on the customer!) He pays specific attention to including how these products and services have benefitted other customers. Joe continues for 15 minutes, making sure to cover every product detail for all he has to offer today.

Sara turned to Steve and commented about the feature of one of the products Joe shared. Steve nodded, and Sara turned to Joe and asked, "If we say, 'yes,' to purchasing this one product today, how soon can you have it delivered?" Joe said, "We'll have it to you on Monday."

"Sounds good. We'll take it!" said Sara. Joe replied, "Great!" He asked Sara for a few details to get the order processed and the delivery scheduled. She and Steve stood and shook hands with Joe, thanking him for coming over today.

Joe was elated as he left the meeting and raced back to the home office to share news of his first sale! He was congratulated on making his first sale and was told to keep up the good work and go make another sale.

The Known and Unknown

It's a common mistake. Little did Joe know when he walked out of his meeting with Sara and Steve, that two things happened. He left *with* something and *without* something. Sure, he left *with* a sale. He also left *without* knowing why!

You could say Joe got lucky. Throughout his features and benefits presentation, he happened to hit on the one thing Sara and Steve were looking for to solve their problem. As far as we know, Joe may not have found out any other way. He never asked them what problems they were facing or what it was they were trying to solve. This lack of curiosity left him in a common communication pitfall of telling and not asking. Joe told them what he had to offer and failed to ask them what they needed.

Like many people new to sales, Joe believed if he shared all the great features and benefits of his products and services, people would want to buy from him.

Let's see how this strategy worked for Joe on his very next sales call.

The Disconnected Connection

Joe arrived at the offices of Century, Inc., one of the most well-known firms in their industry, for his next sales call. Joe was scheduled to meet with the owners, Rocky and Amanda. He was escorted into Rocky's office where they were waiting. After the opening greetings, Joe began to talk about his company and their success in bringing their products and services to market. Before Joe got very far, Rocky started asking him questions.

Normally, this would be the time to answer Rocky's questions specifically and continue to ask questions until Joe fully understood what his prospect wanted to know or solve.

Sadly, Joe did not pick up on that at all. He went right into the features and benefits of his products and services. He covered all the details and then Amanda asked, "Are there other companies using these products?" Joe said, "Yes! These are our most popular products in the marketplace."

Amanda continued, "I'm not sure if these products are going to be right for our needs." Then Rocky said, "We are going to have to think about this some more. Thanks for stopping in. Why don't you give me a call next week?" A little perplexed, Joe said, "OK. I'll reach out to you in the middle of next week. Thanks for your time."

Joe stood and shook hands with them and walked out, wondering what happened.

He sat in his car for a bit before returning to the office. He did exactly what worked last time. Why didn't they buy? He wondered if he missed something. Was there a feature or benefit he inadvertently left out?

Before we begin to address some solutions for what Joe did and didn't do, let me tell you the truth about these stories. They really did happen. I changed the names to protect the innocent, however, I am willing to put my hand up and let you know that these two scenes actually happened to me. I walked out of both experiences not knowing why I succeeded and why I failed. My perspective about what it took to be successful in sales was narrow and self-focused. Not a good combination. The best result from these two experiences was that I began to discover what was missing. There is so much more to unpack, but let's start with some of the missing pieces.

What Was Missing?

When you've experienced a failure to close the sale, it's important to start by asking yourself some of the following questions:

- What was missing?

- Did I ask the right questions?

- Did I say enough?

- Did I say too much?

- Did I miss any signals from my prospect about what they did or did not want?

- Did I uncover what was most important to them?

- Did I ...?"

So many questions can be asked here. Yes, there are times when it may be because of things outside of your control. I have found over the years that the most common missing ingredient for me was the right perspective. I have learned that if my perspective is focused in the wrong place, it won't matter what I say. I am most likely to miss the mark and fail. The truth is that perspective is everything when it comes to sales! Let me show you why the proper perspective is powerful and one of the most important factors in your success.

Knowing your product or service well is important. However, the most important part of the sales process is getting to know your customers and what their needs are. They are most often trying to solve a problem, so your assignment is to be a solution provider. This starts with you asking questions to uncover the specific problem they are trying to solve. If you are going to talk about a feature or benefit of your product or service, keep the focus on what solutions your product or service delivers and if it is the proper solution for their needs. Know this: When you can describe your prospect's problem better than they can, you will turn them into a customer!

It is easier to do most of the talking in a sales presentation. I have done that more times than I care to admit. Over my career, I have also learned why it is the wrong approach to keep talking when communicating with a potential customer. Your focus should not be on what you have to say. It should be on what problem your potential customer is trying to solve.

One of the most effective ways to improve your perspective when meeting with a customer is to be curious. Curiosity leads you to ask more questions, and the prospects' answers help you ask more specific questions that lead to understanding exactly what solution is needed for your prospect.

Perspective – Defined

According to Webster's New World Dictionary, the definition of perspective for our purposes is "*a) a specific point of view in understanding or judging things or events, esp. one that shows them in their true relations to one another, b) the ability to see things in a true relationship. A mental view.*"[3]

It's paramount that we get on the same page with this definition. As we will see throughout this book, it is common for everyone to have their own perspective about what they do and perceive, and how it relates to the big picture. That's because perspective is a personal measure of what we see, know, or understand. For example, we can be standing side-by-side with both of us looking out the same window at the same scene. When asked independently what we were looking at out the window, it would be common to get different perspectives. One might see something specific, like a person walking or the shape of an individual building. The other might observe the bigger picture and see the landscape as a whole, or even notice the mountain range beyond the skyline of the city. Remember, we are both looking out the same window at the same time, yet our perspectives can differ greatly.

What is a Sales Perspective?

If you're in leadership or management for an organization, it's common practice to look at sales as a number: number of products sold, number of services rendered, number of clients or customers, number of policies written, etc. This perspective only considers part of the overall process. Numbers only tell part of the story. If you truly want to understand the important factors that drive sales, you can't look at numbers alone. There are so many ways to think about the idea of sales when formulating your company's sales strategy. The best ways to evaluate the critical elements of your ultimate sales strategy are to open yourself to the whole story.

For example, when you meet someone for the first time, it's common to ask each other what you each do for a living. When the other person tells you they're in sales you don't go, "OK, got it." You are much more likely to ask them additional questions:

- What is your industry?

- Where do you work?

- Do you specialize in or focus on a particular product or service?

- How long have you been in sales?

- What do you like about your career?

- And so on ...

If you are looking at numbers alone, when it comes to sales, your details are limited. You only have a portion of the story. This singular view makes it harder to effectively forecast your future sales because you're only looking at part of the picture of what it takes to truly reach the growth or increase you are seeking.

The Perspective Model

After decades of sitting in meetings with senior leadership, department heads, sales directors, immediate bosses, and my peers, I've developed an understanding of how perspectives differ between management and sales. Choosing the proper perspective is imperative in the sales field. While management typically sees the role of sales differently than those who are actually in the marketplace meeting with prospects and customers, understand that it's not disconnected, just different.

The sales model of measuring numbers is most associated with the Management Perspective—how senior leadership looks at results. The sales model of valuing people is most associated with the Sales Perspective—how the field sales team looks at results.

Perspective Model

Management Perspective	VS	Sales Perspective
CLOSING		CONNECTING
TRANSACTIONS		TRANSFORMATION
RESULTS		RELATIONSHIPS
NUMBERS #		PEOPLE

As you can see in the Perspective Model above, the ultimate focus drives the differing perspectives. When your focus is on the numbers, as it typically is with management, you're always evaluating the tally of how many sales are closed in a given time period. Please understand that I don't dismiss this perspective! Management has an obligation to report on the numbers to the financial team, senior leadership, the Board of Directors, and shareholders. Numbers have become the common measure of growth and profitability. But what if you could use that approach to your advantage and deliver the best numbers by changing your view to the Sales Perspective?

On the sales side, success comes from focusing on building relationships with the people you call on. Rather than strictly counting the numbers, the Sales Perspective leads you to make positive connections with the clients and customers you'll be serving. When you seek to help your client or customer transform their situation from a problem to a solution, you end up building the kind of relationships that will consistently take care of any numbers required of you.

A false or incomplete perspective will limit your understanding and thus your ability to know what's most important to your customer. You must first understand the power of perspective which leads you to embrace the most important element of sales. Numbers alone won't reveal what you need to know to properly value the essential elements of a real sales perspective. You have to dig deeper.

Understanding the Power of Perspective

For decades, books on sales strategy have focused on the skills and abilities needed to effectively close deals. Organizations are always evaluating their sales teams by their capacity to deliver sales results for the company. Beware that the pressure to close deals doesn't outweigh the value delivered to the customer. When closing deals at any cost gets out of balance with building relationships with your customers, the wrong pressure can build in your organization. This type of pressure can lead to a wrong attitude that leads to asking self-serving questions that put your client or customer in a forced position to say yes. This has the potential to be a misguided strategy, especially when it's built on the pressure to hit your sales goals over the needs of the customer.

This book is not about tactics or strategies to close the sale. It's not about helping you manage your schedule so you can get enough calls in to see enough people to close enough deals to meet the sales goals given to you by your company. There are enough resources in the marketplace that provide those details, should you want them.

I want to help you accomplish any goals given to you by showing you how to get your mindset off your sales goals, territory growth, or even the pressure to keep your job.

One of the greatest challenges that people in sales face is managing their attitudes and the built-in pressures that often come along as a package deal with the imposed sales goals from management for the next month, next quarter, or next year.

It's true that when looking at the new parameters and goals given to you, the first view you have is based upon your own perspective.

Are these numbers realistic in the current market?

Will my company be able to deliver the product on time?

What do I need to do to make sure I hit my goals?

How many more clients or customers will I need to find to grow my territory?

With the current state of my competition in the market, what will I need to change to hit my numbers?

The challenge is, if you only look at what *you* need to do in this new sales cycle to hit your goals, you miss out on understanding a critical perspective that can help you accomplish everything you need. In reviewing everything you think you need to do to succeed, it's your perspective that needs to change!

If you never grow beyond your own understanding, you miss out on recognizing the greatest opportunities to serve your clients and customers. Remaining in your own shell keeps you from exploring and learning from those around you.

If you convince yourself that you know what your client or customer wants, you may be right *or* you may be wrong. You will never fully understand their needs if you don't ask them what they want. Assuming what they want without ever mining for the real reason your prospects are seeking a solution is a failed strategy. Thinking that you already know what they want cannot be depended upon or duplicated to drive a sustained outcome as a sales strategy. You may win some and lose some, but you are not building a reliable and duplicatable sales strategy that delivers lasting results.

Turning Point – A Lesson in Perspective

A real turning point for me happened when I transitioned to a Business-to-Business-for-Consumer (B2B4C) sales role as a territory representative for an insurance carrier. My job was to call on independent insurance agencies who sold my company's products to their customers. One of my first agency visits was with the marketing manager of one of our largest agencies. I set up an appointment to visit with Wayne Bogatzki, at Lee F. Murphy Insurance Agency, in St. Paul, MN.

When I went to see Wayne, he came out to the front desk to welcome me. We continued to chat as he led me down the hallway toward his office. He began to tell me about another company representative who had visited him earlier in the day. He stopped in the middle of the hallway and said to me, "You know what I hate? When someone comes into my office and says to me, *'What have you got for me?'* I quickly see that all they are here to do is check my agency off on their call log and ask me to give them what they want. They never stop to ask me what I want. I usually don't have much to give to someone like that."

I nodded in agreement. As we proceeded to his office, I made the commitment to myself right there to never say the words, 'What have you got for me?' to any of my clients!

Wayne and I have developed a great relationship over the years, and we wrote a lot of business together. I admire and respect him as a businessman and as a person. I had the privilege of having lunch with him years later and I shared this story with him and thanked him for the impact he had on me from our first meeting years earlier. He was genuinely pleased and smiled as we talked about the importance of relationships in business.

I shared with him the strategy I had developed by asking a probing question this way: *"What are you working on that I might be able to help you with so you can hit your goals this quarter?"*

I told him my goal was to make sure that my client knew my focus was on helping them with their needs. He smiled and said, "Absolutely. That's it!"

Notice the difference between these two sentences:

1. What have you got for me?
Vs.
2. What are you working on that I can help you with so you can accomplish your goals this quarter?

As you see in the first sentence, when you end your statement with *me*, that is what your client identifies as your primary focus. Nobody likes or even respects someone who is only there to take from them. You may be a very likable person, but you can sabotage your relationships when your focus is only on yourself and your own needs.

In the second sentence, notice that although "I" was used once, it was surrounded with four "you" references! The purpose is to make sure your message conveys your ultimate intentions. Make it clear to them that your desire is to help them accomplish what they want.

When you set out to help someone solve their problems or meet their goals you will begin building a lasting relationship that will deliver the kind of value that sets you apart from your competition. Examine yourself with this question:

> *Do you want to become dependable or disposable to your clients?*

Remember, the remnants of what you say and do can linger in their minds after you leave and help to solidify their experience with you—good or bad. Make it your goal to leave them with a positive experience after each connection. It's your job to help them recognize the value you bring to their business through each sales experience.

The Most Important Perspective

The secret that you will learn in this book is that the most important perspective in every sales experience is that of the ultimate customer. It doesn't matter if your sales model is Business-to-Consumer (B2C), Business-to-Business (B2B), or Business-to-Business-for-Consumer (B2B4C). In my experience, knowing and understanding what the customer wants takes precedence over every other perspective.

How do I know this?

How have I come to this conclusion?

Where does my insight and perspective come from?

I have been actively involved in sales since the 1980s. In fact, in the year 2024, I marked 43 years in sales, and I can assure you that I am not basing my conclusions on theory or someone else's ideas. I have done what all great salespeople do: I take input and structure from others who are successful and personalize it. I make mistakes. I learn from them. I commit to continual growth personally and professionally. One of the greatest characteristics of a sales professional is not to recite a specific script, but instead, take the method or framework you choose and make it your own.

Learning from the wisdom, insight, and experience of others is always helpful. Don't ever try to go it alone in sales. I have made it a habit to read and learn from others every chance I get. This desire to keep learning and growing has helped me to recognize the pressure placed upon me for results was not the secret to sales success.

The motivation to close more deals means you are always chasing another opportunity and not taking the time to slow down and get to know the customers that you have gained. You don't even realize you are missing a great opportunity to win new customers by building relationships with your current customers. The big disconnect is missing out on really knowing what is most important to your customer.

Over time, I came to realize that assuming what the customer valued most was a grave mistake. So, I set out on a journey to shift my selling strategy away from my goals and my demands. I started learning the most effective ways to uncover what my clients and customers really wanted.

In his book, *Know What You're FOR*, author Jeff Henderson points us directly to the crux of the ultimate business focus when he acknowledges that every organization needs to grow. Henderson says, "Growth may look different, but it's something we all should want. Knowing this, what causes a business to grow? Sure, there are lots of answers, but ultimately it comes down to one word—*customers.*" This perspective is more than sentiment. It is the key to unlocking your business strategy. When you set your focus on understanding what's most important to your customers, your organization's growth becomes a natural by-product of serving your customer's needs first. Henderson goes on to say, "We must learn to care more for the customer than we care for the business. We must learn to care more about people than about the organization. This isn't bad for business because customers *are* the business. Caring for the customer creates an emotional bond that allows them to care more about the business." [4]

Take just a moment and re-read the previous four sentences from Jeff Henderson. It's possible that if you're like me, this perspective about the customer may seem a bit bold. If you take the time to pause and reflect, you may gain the clarity that leads you to a renewed energy about what's most important in your business.

Planting Seeds

Have you ever been in a meeting where you present a new idea to the group and everyone in the room gets it except one person, and that one person happens to be the decision-maker?

I was invited by a young agent and his manager from one of my largest clients to present the details of a self-insured workers' compensation program to one of their prospective customers. That meeting consisted of the two agents, the prospect's HR director, safety manager, the owner of the company, and me. After I shared the details and benefits of the program I represented, everyone in the room had a clear understanding of the program except the owner. She struggled with embracing this new idea as the correct solution for the company to address their challenges. Granted, it was a different solution to the standard insurance they had purchased for years. The HR Director and the Safety Manager not only saw the benefits of the program to their company, but they also began lobbying the owner to move forward with this program.

As the objections kept coming from the owner, I was reminded of a lesson I had learned long ago that there are times when some ideas, though they may be clear to some, may also be like higher math to others. If it seems as though I am speaking about geometry, algebra, or even calculus, I must remember to simplify it as much as possible. In other words, I need to stick to addition and subtraction by keeping my examples and questions clear and straightforward and forgo anything that complicates or confuses the message.

In this case, I continued to ask questions to better understand what was behind the objections that the owner was raising. Was there something unsaid that was driving the inability to listen to her managers about the benefits this program would bring to the company? As I continued to simplify the message, the owner was at least willing to think more about it and committed to getting back to us with a decision the following week.

When we left the meeting, the agents thanked me for a job well done in handling what seemed to them as unreasonable push-back on the benefits this program offered their prospect. I reminded them sometimes we can be ready for a prospect, but they may not be ready for us. The opposite can also be true. Someone may be ready to join this program, but we aren't ready for them until they address some challenges with their operation. Either way, our goal is to find where opportunity and preparedness meet and always keep our focus on the customer's perspective. If they don't get it right away and are not willing to change, the best thing we can do is plant the seed of an idea with them and let it grow over time.

The following week, the agent called to tell me that the owner decided not to go with the program we presented. I told him that I understood and that this program is an idea that takes time for some people to grasp. Maybe they'll be ready next year.

Wait for It

One day, I received a call from the young agent in the story above. I had moved on to another company since we presented to that prospect and although I was no longer representing the program, the agent called me to say, "Thank you!"

I asked him what for, and he told me that he had just written the business with that owner who finally came around to the value in the program I had presented two years earlier. The agent said in his conversation with his new customer that the seed of influence planted from our first conversation two years ago had an impact which allowed the owner to warm up to the idea in her own time. The agent had stayed in touch with them a couple of times each year since we first presented to them and was invited to have a shot at their business this year. The agent wanted to thank me for planting the seed two years earlier as it was instrumental in helping his customer make the best decision for their business.

I was struck by the importance of leaving a positive influence in the marketplace, whether I benefited or not, that allowed the agent to win with their customer and allow the customer to ultimately win with a needed solution for their business.

After the call, I was happy for the agent and the customer as they had built a partnership that would benefit them both. Even though I would not be part of the business relationship going forward, the seed of influence that was planted years earlier allowed both parties to win. I found myself honored to have received the call and recognized the importance of serving others regardless of the outcome.

This reinforced one of the most importance sales strategies you can implement in your business:

- *Help your customer win!*

or (as in the story above)

- *Help your client win with their customer!*

Don't forget it. This perspective will help you drive lasting impact in your business. The difference you will make each time you strive to help someone else win, may be evident at the time, or may appear sometime down the road. You won't always know. Focus on planting seeds that help others win and you will never lose.

Sales Perspective Habits

Start
- Recognize that there is more than one perspective in a sales experience.

Analyze
- Know your products and services well *and* study your customer's perspective and their potential needs.

Learn
- Stop the benefits spill! Ask questions to learn what your prospect is looking for or what problem they are trying to solve.

Engage
- Be curious. Let their answers to your initial questions lead you to more specific questions and a deeper understanding of their needs.

Serve
- Keep your focus on them as the most important perspective in the conversation.
- Serve them buy adding value to their business.

THE PERSPECTIVE MINDSET

REDEFINING WIN-WIN

"Help others achieve their dreams and you will achieve yours." [5]

— Les Brown

The Big Picture (See the Landscape beyond Your Own Goals)

As with any journey, it's important to look at the big picture. Without seeing things from a larger view, it's easy to get sidetracked and run off on small tangents or stay solely focused on what's right in front of you.

In sales, it's easy to get caught up in focusing on the goals laid before you regarding your own territory. Sometimes these goals are the result of a collaborative process and sometimes you're just told what your goals are for the year and then it's up to you to figure out how you're going to hit your numbers.

If your only focus is your own goals, you will miss the opportunities to make connections and drive value to your clients and their customers.

I have learned over the years not to overreact to the goals I'm given but look up from my goals and see the landscape around me. When I start to see the big picture, including everyone else's needs, then I can put my goals in perspective.

Knowing what you want to accomplish is important.

- Yes, I want to hit or exceed my goals.

- Yes, I want to honor my employer.

- Yes, I want to serve my clients and customers.

- Yes, I want to be successful in my endeavors.

Over the years, I have discovered the best way to achieve what I want is to first focus on helping others get what they want. I like the way Dale Carnegie states it in his book, *How to Win Friends and Influence People.* In chapter three, under Fundamental Techniques in Handling People, Carnegie says,

"So the only way on earth to influence other people is to talk about what *they* want and show them how to get it." [6]

You'll find the best way to know, understand, and embrace the big picture is to clarify some important definitions. This is not solely about changing your thinking, it's about clarifying your ideas and building a common ground of understanding.

As you look to drive value in the big picture, you must first come to a new understanding of what WIN-WIN really means. The general idea of WIN-WIN has to do with the mutual benefit to both parties. I've seen the idea of WIN-WIN used in such a way where the focus is not on your customer, but on your ultimate personal victories. This is a flawed strategy. I believe there's a better way to look at this that will maximize the valued benefit you bring to your clients.

Redefining WIN-WIN: A New Definition

Let's examine how a new perspective on this old idea can transform your relationships and your results! A common view of WIN-WIN in the marketplace is the following:

- You scratch my back, and I'll scratch yours.

- You take care of me, and I'll take care of you.

- You give me what I want, and I'll give you what you want.

- You give me the shirt off your back, and ... I'll have it cleaned and pressed before returning it to you (or something like that)!

Notice that in the traditional sense, WIN-WIN is about you getting your needs met first. It is also interesting to note that the conjunctive use of "and" has a hidden meaning that assumes the addition of the word "then" after it.

- You scratch my back and (then) I'll scratch yours.

- You take care of me and (then) I'll take care of you.

- You give me what I want and (then) I'll give you what you want, etc.

It plays out as an implied, "me first – you second" approach. Truly not a serving posture, but rather, a self-serving posture. This is not an effective way to build relationships.

So, what if...

What would happen in your life if you turned this whole idea on its head? What if you chose to put someone else first? What would it be like to put their interests ahead of your own? I know this is a radical idea. I know this is counter-intuitive for most people, especially in sales. That is why you must try it!

The idea of my helping someone else first—helping them get what they want *before* I get what I want—seriously? Yes, seriously!

If you don't want to be like everyone else out there, if you want to stand out and win in a unique way, then you need to try this new strategy.

I would like to introduce you to a new definition of WIN-WIN:

I'll help you get what you want ... and eventually I'll win.

It goes something like this:

- I'll scratch your back ...

- I'll take care of your needs ...

- I'll give you what you want ...

- I'll give you the shirt off my back ...

I'm sure you're wondering why I didn't finish the sentences above. In the redefined world of WIN-WIN, I did. Once I made a change in my mindset to only consider the other person's point of view, I realized I didn't need to be concerned about my side of the narrative. Let me explain.

Mindset Adjustment

Change happened in my results when I converted my thinking to make it a priority to focus on my client's perspective. Once I made this shift, everything took off. My new mindset began to transform when I adjusted my self-talk. My mental dialogue, as if speaking to my customer, started out like this:

> "The real key here starts with my thinking. I must think about your needs, period. If I start with you and keep my focus on helping you accomplish your goals, and if I work tirelessly and selflessly to bring you to where you want to go, you will look at me as a giver and not a taker. Therefore, I will seek to learn what it is that you want. I will strive to help you get it. I will

> *put your needs first in my thinking and my actions. I will join you as a partner on your journey and always give my best to you."*

The freedom I gained in striving to help my clients and customers win first took all the pressure off my other concerns. Over time, as I began to master the art of helping other people win, my numbers always took care of themselves!

This is a transformative idea for you and for those around you. When others see you as someone who serves, they will recognize you in a different light. The key difference may not be solely in how they view you, but in how they view you in comparison to your competition.

We will put this idea to use in the upcoming chapters and show you just how effective it can be in driving your results to new levels.

The "Eyes" Have It

Here is another concept to help you refine your thinking. *Take your eyes off yourself and put them on other people.* You will be amazed at the outcome.

What does it really mean to take your eyes off yourself?

Think about it this way. You get ready in the morning and look in the mirror to make sure your hair is in place, or your outfit looks good, etc. Then your mind shifts to thinking what you see in the mirror is what your customers or clients will see when you meet with them today. You pause, and ask yourself this question aloud, "Is there more to me than what they'll see from my appearance?" Of course, the answer is yes!

Consider your social media presence. You are quickly judged by your profile picture, yet that is only a snapshot of who you are. Your hope is that people will read your tag line, content, or bio to learn more about you, which may cause them to reach out and connect.

Remember, your appearance is only part of the first impression. It only tells part of your story. Yes, you dress professionally and care about yourself and your appearance, but this is only a glimpse of who you are. It doesn't tell the whole story. It's not the full impression of who you are, what you have to say, what you do, how you do it, and the value you bring to every connection.

When you start thinking beyond the first impression you have of your customer, you begin to realize there is also more to them than what you initially see. You have some discoveries to make to get to know the full story about your customer and their needs.

Taking your eyes off yourself and putting them on other people starts with a change in your focus from what you want to what someone else wants. Make this your first move and you will succeed. Make their needs your priority. When you help someone else first, even if they don't directly return the favor or service, you will still be farther ahead in life. The key is to operate in your new WIN-WIN mindset and find ways to help *them* win.

Watch Out for Land Mines!

Taking the wrong step when trying to make a first impression can be disastrous. One of the greatest battles we face with ourselves every day is taking the business-as-usual approach. We get caught up in thinking or even saying, "This is how we've always done it!" When that happens (believe me it has happened to me, many times), I find myself missing the mark completely or at minimum not connecting with my client.

Don't get hung up in an old pattern that can lose its luster with your clients and cause them to think of you in a "same old" model. This can lead to an openness in your client's mind to new ideas they hear from *someone else*. You should be the one opening their minds to new ideas, not someone else! Don't leave this to chance. Be on your game and continue to think about ways you can bring strategies and solutions to them that meet their needs!

Don't Be an Empty Suit

Years ago, I had received a phone call from someone I had never met before. I was in training at my company's regional office when I received a call from an agency owner requesting my assistance in resolving an issue he was having with one of the departments in my new company. He shared with me what was happening, and I told him I would investigate and get back to him with an answer. The next day I confirmed the answer from my company and called him back to update him on our policy and how this issue would be resolved. He thanked me for getting to the bottom of this and he looked forward to meeting me once I got going in the territory.

Two weeks later, when I was back home in Minnesota, I set up an appointment to introduce myself to Ted Rogers of Casualty Assurance, in Chaska, MN. He welcomed me into his office and asked that we chat before meeting the rest of his team. He was a man of vast experience, and I asked him about his business. I enjoyed learning about how he started his own agency and worked his way up to where he was today. Before our meeting was over, he shared with me something that has had a profound impact on me.

Ted said, "When I called you and we talked while you were still at your regional office for training, I asked for some assistance in resolving a matter. You took my call, got the information, and committed to getting an answer and get back to me the next day. I was pleased to receive a call from you the next day as promised, and you also provided a resolution to my problem. I have people in sales that come into my office on a regular basis. Some are problem-solvers, and some are empty suits.

"Some will come and chat with me, drink my coffee, talk with my staff, and take up their time as well. They never really add any value to what we do here. They just show up and talk and leave. They are empty suits.

"You are not an empty suit. You are a problem-solver, and I appreciate that about you. You took my call, made a commitment to get back to me and then followed through. We are going to get along just fine. Please get us on your calendar on a regular basis. We will be glad to work with you. Thanks for caring about my business."

I walked out of Ted's office that day recognizing the importance of having a positive impact on someone by simply making a commitment and then following through. I know it's hard to believe not everyone does this consistently, yet it's important to note that everyone has an impact on their client or customer.

Don't mistake activity for value. Whether we think we have accomplished anything with our clients or not is irrelevant! If they consider us to be an empty suit, then we will bring a burden to their office. Oh, we will have an impact all right. It just won't be the kind that welcomes us back again and again.

If you want to have a positive impact on your clients, don't be an empty suit. Serve your client's interests and follow through with the value you promise. You will be a problem-solver in their eyes and be welcome in their office any time.

Sales Perspective Habits

Start
- Let the idea of redefining WIN-WIN sink in. Start helping other people win and don't worry about the rest.

Analyze
- Read and repeat the newly defined WIN-WIN narrative: I'll scratch your back...etc. Let the unfinished statement guide you to a new understanding of taking care of your customer.

Learn
- Examine times when your efforts were focused on closing the sale rather than helping your customer win. Let your past mistakes guide you to putting your customers' needs first.

Engage
- Take your eyes off yourself and focus on the outcome your customer wants.

Serve
- Don't be an empty suit. Make commitments, follow up, and follow through!

CLOSE THE GAP

OVERCOME THE DISCONNECT, ELIMINATE ASSUMPTIONS AND GET TO THE HEART OF THE MATTER

> *"The best salespeople wonder what it would be like to be in the other person's shoes. They know they can't play that game unless they continually strive to train themselves in how we as human beings communicate."*[7]
>
> — Bob Phibbs

Communication Games

DO YOU REMEMBER PLAYING the "Telephone Game" when you were growing up? It's the game that starts out simply and then, quickly turns into an often unpredictable, confusing, and humorous outcome. For those that may not know the game, or may have called it by a different name, here's how it's played:

You start with a group of people arranged in a straight line. For larger groups you can form a circle. The greater the number of people the greater the fun. Let's say there are ten people playing. Once you form a line, make sure that people are far enough apart that the others around them cannot hear what is being said. The player who starts turns to the next person in line and whispers in their ear a word, statement, or phrase with specific details. It doesn't have to be long and drawn out, it simply needs to be specific. For example, you might say something like, "I went to the grocery store to buy eggs, bananas, butter, biscuits, and bread."

The person who first receives this information turns to the next person in line and attempts to pass on the information by whispering what they recall from what they just heard. The game continues as each person receives the information and then whispers what they recall to the next person in line until the last person receives the statement shared.

Although it seems like a harmless sentence, you'd be surprised how many people mix up the different items you went to purchase. It's also common to drop an item from the list or fail to keep them all separate. When the last person has been told the sentence, they announce what they think they heard. Next, the person who started it off states what they shared to the second person. This is where the fun begins as people laugh and enjoy the great difference between how the statement started and how it ended! For example, the listener may get the b-words and drop eggs off the list or turn "butter, biscuits" into "buttered biscuits," or even have the list turn into just one or two items.

This game often reflects how important it is to know, understand, and remember the details in each of your encounters with your clients and customers. I have always found it helpful to remind myself that the details are important, and I should do my best to remember what a customer wants and why it's important to *them*. Knowing the 'what' and the 'why' as defined by the customer, allows me to measure how my product or service might provide a solution to their needs.

The Heart of the Matter

So often, we find ourselves pursuing an outcome that *we* want because our focus is on ourselves. In sales, it could mean hitting your monthly goals, earning a bonus, qualifying for a special promotion, etc. It could even be as simple as earning enough to make your house payment this month. Depending on our circumstances, our motivations may vary.

As you learned in the last chapter, when you focus on yourself, you risk missing what's important to your customer. This is the real heart of the matter. You need to recognize this isn't about you at all!

It's about the customer. Period.

The only thing that really matters when it comes to your preparation, engagement, and follow-through in any encounter with your clients and customers is their perspective.

How do you make sure your energy and effort are focused on the right things? It starts with identifying your role in the process. Knowing this will drive the details of your actions.

The Differentiator

What is the differentiator? What is the one thing that sets your results apart from others in the field? What is the special sauce? We are all looking for the edge, the thing that makes us special, unique, of highest value to our customer.

In her book, *Changing the Sales Conversation,* Linda Richardson identifies the key to differentiation in today's sales environment. Right out of the gate in her introduction, Richardson says, "Differentiation is not your products. It is your expertise. You have become the differentiator." [8]

That definition is convincingly clear in its simplicity. Read it again before going on! This concept is the key to understanding your role in sales. It applies to the three primary sales roles in today's marketplace: Business-to-Consumer (B2C), Business-to-Business (B2B), and Business-to-Business-for-Consumer (B2B4C) or representative sales.

I have had jobs in all three of the above-mentioned sales positions. Over the last 21 years, my primary role has been in B2B4C, where I've worked as a territory sales representative for an insurance company. My job was to call on independent insurance agencies who sold my company's products and services to their customers. I helped them with training and product knowledge and helped them prepare to sell the overall value of the products I represented. Just as I have represented my company's products and services to my clients, they in turn sell my products and services to meet the needs of their customers.

In a representative sales role, it is unusual for you to meet with the ultimate customer. *This is where you can become the differentiator!* The approach you take helps you define how you serve your clients *and* the ultimate customer. When you think beyond your client and help them connect with their customer, you'll take your game to the next level. Here is where you help put your client in the best position to win with their customer, and you'll set yourself apart in the industry.

Your success has everything to do with how you approach the transaction. Typically, in B2B4C selling, you will not get to participate in the closing of the sale. The primary reason is you are not normally invited to the presentation of the quote or proposal. So, how do you approach the transaction? What's your strategy? You do have a strategy, don't you? Are you just going through the motions of a benefits spill with your client hoping that something sticks?

Rick Larson, co-founder of the leading real estate and insurance licensure training company in St. Paul, MN, is a former boss of mine and great mentor to me. Rick taught me many important lessons. One helped me learn how to gather data to make the best decision when facing a challenge. In his common baseball coach vernacular, he used to say, "We have to go all the way around the bases to gather all the information we need to know before making a decision." He stressed the importance of knowing all the options so the best decision can be made for the situation.

As a result of this strategy, I have been a big believer that *the best decisions are made from the best information.* Going "all around the bases" has become a standard pattern for me in assessing a situation and then pausing to gather data and gain insight into what's ahead. This process allows me to identify the best decisions and strategies I can deliver to my clients and keeps me from acting impulsively or emotionally.

PERSPECTIVE Time Out ⏰

– Be careful not to get caught in the trap of making decisions while you are in an emotional state.

EXAMPLE: You have just been notified that you were not awarded the contract on a large project for your client. It went to one of your competitors because they brought a level of detail to one aspect of the process that resonated with the customer. You know that your product and service in this area is superior to your competition, and you immediately feel like your team let you down in the delivery of the details of your program. STOP! This is not the time to point fingers. This is the time for self-reflection. What could you have done differently? How was your value proposition delivered and why was it delivered "incomplete" to your client? Who's responsible? (FYI-You are!)

This is the time to review all aspects of your sales process. How you gather data, who is responsible for delivering on the different aspects of your value proposition, how you put it all together for your client, etc.

Losing out on a sale can be one of the best value lessons you encounter because it challenges you to answer the following questions.

- *Did I do all that I could have done for my client?*

- *What was missing?*

- *Does any component of my product or program need additional attention?*

- *Have I done everything possible to maximize the value in the things I can control?*

- *Are there any questions we missed that should have been asked?*

Review Time

When you engage in the journey of walking through your presentation in review, you gain the opportunity to fine tune aspects that can be strengthened for the next opportunity.

This is also the best time to perform a spot check review. When possible, check in with your client about the process and review what happened or didn't happen in the presentation. Connect with your internal team to discuss options you didn't pursue because of time, information, etc. Determine how you can actively get ahead of the process in the future by gathering the necessary data far enough in advance so your team can deliver at their highest level.

You will be amazed that going around the bases and gathering all the data to make any necessary adjustments will typically lead you to the affirmation of the things you are doing well *and* identify areas of opportunity to strengthen your strategy for better results going forward.

Why is maximizing the value you bring to your client important? Let's examine a new way to view your client and prospect or customer that can help you bring a new level of value.

Who's Who?

The terms client and customer are often used interchangeably in the marketplace. In B2C and B2B sales it's common to describe the end user as the customer. They are in effect the purchaser or buyer of a product or service they will use.

In B2B4C, or representative sales, it's more likely that the person selecting your product will turn and remarket or sell your product or service to their customer. In this case they function as a dealer or agent and not the end user of your product or service. It's been my experience that the following two definitions are important and not as interchangeable as most people think.

A *Client* is a person or group that uses the professional advice or services of a lawyer, accountant, advertising agency, architect, etc. A *Customer* is a person who purchases goods or services from another; buyer; patron. [9]

When you are not directly connected to the end user of your product or service you must act as a sales consultant when partnering with your client (dealer, agent, etc.).

I am spending time here with the representative sales model because in today's business climate, some business owners will delegate certain vetting or curating responsibilities to others on their behalf. When you are dealing with a representative of the owner, who is not the ultimate decision-maker, you'll need to adjust your strategy in communicating effectively with this new representative. Start thinking of them as your client and help them communicate the specifics of the value you and your products and services bring to the business owner's specific needs.

A Quick Lesson in Representative Selling

Out of curiosity, I had a conversation with one of my clients recently and I asked him if he'd ever gone to meet with a prospect, only to have the business owner redirect him to connect with someone else at his company who'd be handling the intake for anyone wanting to quote his insurance business. He told me that yes, he had an experience where he found himself dealing with a designated risk manager who would be gathering information from a number of suitors and then presenting his findings to the owner for a decision. My client said that he was silently frustrated that he wouldn't be dealing with the ultimate decision maker. This situation had him working on the best way he could stand out from any competition he would face. I smiled and acknowledged to him that he now has a glimpse of my role in our relationship. This opened the door for a very interesting conversation as we discussed some of the strategies that I have employed in successfully helping my clients win with their customers.

To proceed effectively, you must make sure you are closing the closest gap to you. Make sure there are no assumptions or misunderstandings between you and your client. When you have their buy-in, you can make specific progress on getting to the heart of the matter, which is focusing on what matters most to the prospect or customer.

Remember, in B2B4C sales, we may never meet the ultimate customer in the transaction. We most often deal directly with the intermediate party and depend on that sales agent or representative to close the deal, make the sale and complete the transaction. If that's the case, how can we have any influence on the actual transaction or sale?

Close the GAP

To properly close the gap, you must first identify what the gap is. In most cases, where there is a gap between you and the prospect or customer, the gap is in understanding how to communicate the value of the product or service you represent. Hold on, let's look deeper!

The initial problem with the gap is we tend to assign value to what the customer needs. The actual gap many sales reps need to overcome is the Generally Assumed Problem (GAP) that your prospect or customer faces. Understand that one of the biggest mistakes you can make in sales is assuming you know the problem your customer or prospect is trying to solve, without ever asking them for their input. *How can you possibly know what they're looking for if you never ask them?*

Because you typically aren't involved directly in the conversation in representative selling, you have no ability to ask follow-up questions to gain additional clarity regarding the problem the ultimate customer is trying to solve.

I have been in representative selling (B2B4C) as a territory/field representative for three different insurance carriers, where I represented my company's products to my clients (insurance agents) who sold my products to their customers (policyholders). Two of the three companies I represented were standard commercial lines carriers. This meant I was only given the opportunity to meet the customer a few times a year. It turned out to be a great challenge to help the agent win with their customer, even though I seldom got to meet or know the ultimate customer. I began to look at this as a new opportunity. I'd ask myself:

- What is the GAP in understanding what the prospect wants?

- Are there barriers between me and my client?

- Are there barriers between my client and their prospect or customer?

- How can I effectively and efficiently close the GAP?

Let's look at a classic example of where the GAP is and why you need to deepen your understanding to overcome it. Your ability to be curious and seek clarity will help you overcome the GAP when you are not in a position to meet with the prospect or customer. In the diagram below, when I connect with my client and my story is based upon a Generally Assumed Problem (GAP) that his prospect has, then my advice may put my client in a position to completely miss the mark when trying to convey the solution to an assumed problem. This means the GAP may remain in place and my client's ability to connect his story to the customers reality will be a challenge. Unfortunately, too many people walk into meetings assuming they know what's best for their prospects without ever taking the time to find out what matters most to them. This GAP, if left unaddressed, will be a roadblock to bonding with your prospect. They will think you don't care about them, their business, or what problem they are trying to solve.

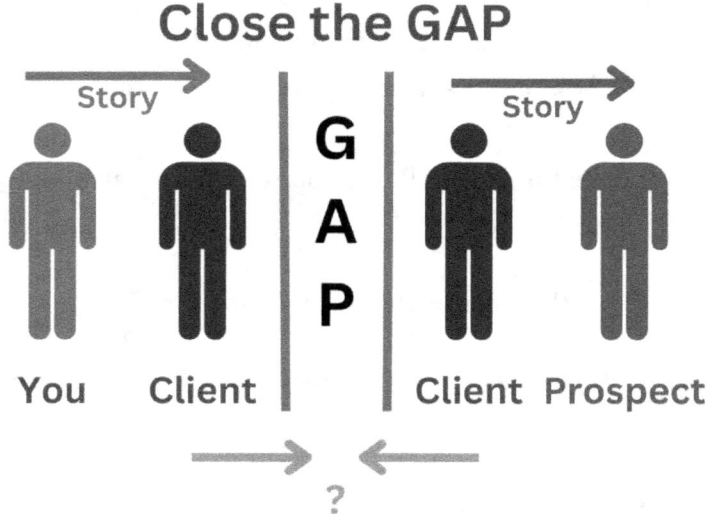

On the left side of the diagram, the story I share with my client is based on my assumption of the prospect's problem. This means communication is split into two entirely different conversations. The story I tell my client may not assist them in connecting with the prospect and may even lead to a major disconnect as they attempt to build a connected relationship. "Close the GAP" means eliminating the barrier that separates connected communication. But how?

I came to realize that I needed a more thorough approach if I was going to deliver on my ability to add value to my client, even when I wasn't present for their meeting with the prospect. Because I was not part of the client-prospect conversation, I became dependent on my agent to share the message of how my products delivered the solution the customer needed. I found the best way for me to deliver the key information to my client, to put them in a position to win, was when I got to know the biggest challenges their customer was likely to face. This allowed me to discuss the important questions my client needed to ask in order to gain a clear understanding of the biggest challenge their prospect was facing.

Once the client understands the challenge, they can determine the right solution to bring to their prospect or customer. This is where doing your homework as a sales representative pays off. When you stay focused on the discovery narrative of asking questions to gain clarity, you avoid the challenge of the Telephone Game. Don't assume anything. Ask and clarify as you go, and you will be in the best position to uncover the most important needs of your customer (more on this topic in Chapter 8).

Get to Know your Client's Customer (even if you never meet them)

In representative sales, if my primary goal is to help my client win, then I need to understand their customer so I can maximize the value I bring to the agent. What I want to know is how my product or service best meets the needs of my client's customer!

I learn to close the GAP by thinking through the target. When I see my direct contact (client/agent) as my target, I want my client's prospect or customer to listen to them and recognize them as a partner to their business. With my focus on the ultimate customer, even if I never meet them, I'm able to empower my client with a specific strategy that increases their opportunity to be seen as the partner their customer is looking for. When that happens, the customer wins. When the customer wins, the agent wins. When the agent wins, they come back to me and say, "Let's do it again!"

Up the Ante on Your Value Proposition

If you want to have a powerful impact on a conversation you're not invited to, this is the key that makes all the difference. Take your Value Proposition to the next level! In B2B4C sales, your value proposition isn't delivered until it gets all the way to your client's customer. You must think in terms of the clear transference of value based upon what the ultimate customer needs. Your ability to help your client win with their customer is based upon your understanding of what your client is up against in trying to earn the trust and win the business with this prospective customer.

Some of my greatest success came when I stopped thinking about the transaction. Don't think in terms of the sale. Think in terms of the transference of value. Make sure you are filling the needs of the customer in ways that maximize the delivery and understanding of the value they are seeking. Shift your thinking from transaction to outcome.

Speak to your client in a language they can repeat to their customer that clarifies the valued outcome in the decision. Once the client uncovers exactly what their customer needs, the best solution reveals itself. Keep your client and customer focused on how this decision delivers the solution the customer is looking for.

- **Value Proposition:** Uncover what their greatest need is and determine if your product or service meets or exceeds their need. Focus on how your offer delivers the outcome they are after!

- **You:** Deliver the value proposition to your client – Be Clear and Concise

- **Client:** Turn and deliver value to the customer – Outcome-based Solutions

- **Customer:** Receive, understand, and embrace value.

Closing the GAP is a 3-Step process.

#1 – Identify the customer's most important need.

#2 – Focus on their need as you communicate, and the GAP will shrink.

#3 – Your story becomes their story.

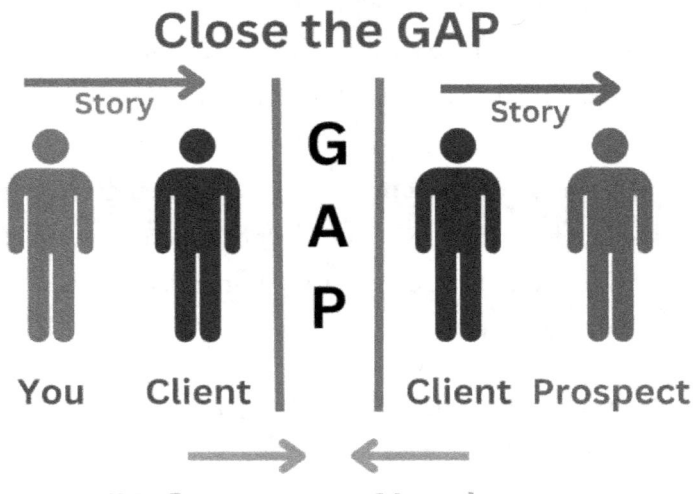
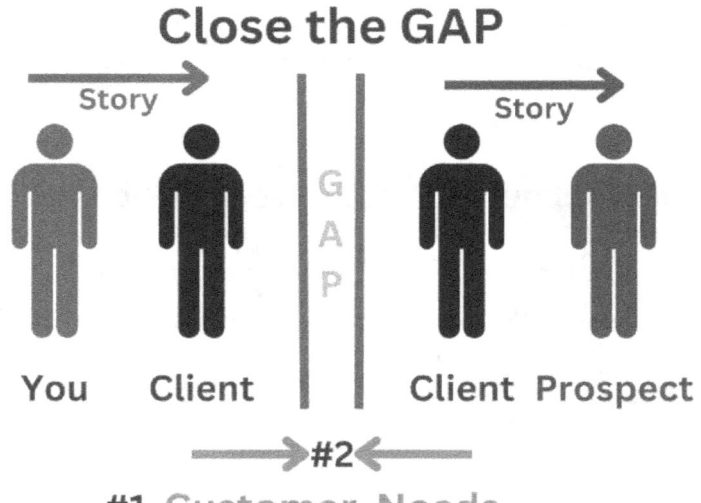

Once I was able to get to the bottom of what their customer may be experiencing, I was able to provide more specific guidance to my client and put them in a position to ask better questions. Typically these questions were focused on getting details about the specific problem the prospect was trying to solve. The GAP started to close when my client kept digging to uncover the specific needs of their prospect.

If you take the time to gather the correct information before you meet with your client, you'll be in the best position to guide them on how to handle their upcoming contact with their prospect. This is the key to closing the GAP. Make the discovery of the customer's needs your highest priority. This posture will also put you in a great position to be perceived as someone who is actually interested in what the customer wants. Believe it or not, this puts you in a rare position that allows you to stand out from the crowd.

Transferring Value

As identified above, the best way to close the gap in understanding and ensure your story is delivered properly is to speak in clear and concise language. Because you're not there to say it, empower your client with the tools that make the flow of information as easy as possible.

As in the diagram above, your ability to close the GAP in the conversation is fully dependent on understanding and embracing your customer's needs. Your value proposition lands clearly in their minds when you tailor it to the specific issues they are trying to solve.

Same Rules

In Business-to-Consumer (B2C) sales, the challenge is the same. If you don't invest time in getting to know what your customer wants most or worse yet, assume what they want, you'll never fully understand their story and the GAP will remain.

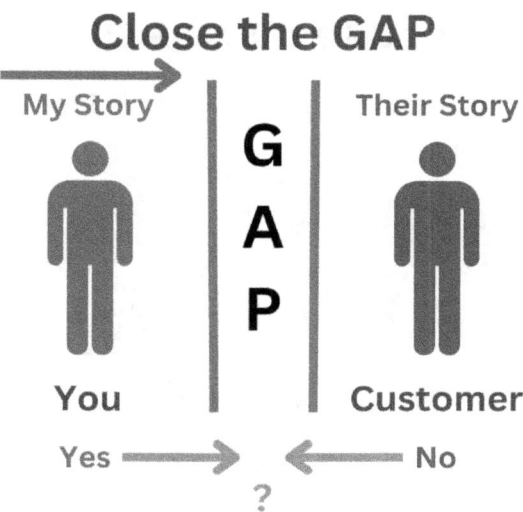

The good news is the rules are also the same. Apply the 3-step process as the key to closing the GAP and discovering a communication connection!

Move Beyond Top-Of-Mind

Often in sales, the over-arching strategy is to position your solution as being top-of-mind with your prospect meaning you are the first resource they look to. This is especially true when the decision is to be made at a later date.

Rather than striving to get top-of-mind status, how would you like to learn the winning strategy that will leave you standing as the only true option for them to consider? In the upcoming chapters I will show you the five steps that will set you so far above the competition that it will ultimately eliminate any other options from the mind of the customer.

Sales Perspective Habits

Start
- Begin today to close the GAP on any assumptions you have made about your prospect, their business, and their challenges.

Analyze
- Acknowledge and own the times that you have moved ahead based upon assumptions.

Learn
- Let the questions you ask your prospects help you define what WIN means to them.

Engage
- With a fresh perspective on helping your customers WIN as your primary objective, ask them to be as specific as possible.

Serve
- Commit to serving their needs above any directive you have been given. Let them know you are there for them by your attitude and your actions.

4
STOP TRYING TO CLOSE THE SALE

LET CURIOSITY LEAD YOU —
UNCOVER WHAT THEY WANT AND GIVE THEM ACCESS TO IT

"Approach each customer with the idea of helping him or her to solve a problem or achieve a goal, not of selling a product or service." [10]

— Brian Tracy

The Language of Sales

WORDS MATTER. WHAT YOU say is important. It is often the difference between just talking to someone and connecting with them. No one ever wants to come off as *salesy* or *pushy*. People tend to bristle at someone who is trying to talk them into making a decision or a purchase. Their defenses go up which ultimately prohibits the type of connection the salesperson is trying to make.

So, how do you adjust your narrative to include the type of language that engages the people you talk to? It starts with strategically setting aside your own goals, responsibilities, and desires. When you make this change it allows you to start focusing on the customer. Once you understand that they care more about their pressures or goals than yours, you'll gain a clearer understanding that they are mostly concerned with finding a solution to *their* issues. When your customer's concerns become foremost in your mind, you are on your way to making the kind of connection that makes a difference in your ability to deliver the valued solution they are looking for in a person, product, or service.

It's certain if you are in sales that you have plenty to be concerned about, however, the language you use, the questions you ask, and the heart of your curiosity will all allow you to ask better questions. Better questions for yourself about your strategy. Better questions for your prospect to learn what's most important to them. Your best strategy is to shift the emphasis in your questioning. It's time to upgrade from the standard questioning that only leads to a shallow understanding of what your customer really wants.

Will the Real Answer Please Stand Up?

Believe it or not, when you ask a standard question, your customer or prospect is more likely to give you a standard answer, much in the same way they responded to a similar question from your competition. This doesn't help you create enough differentiation, especially when your question may be just like something they've already heard from someone else. I want you to learn how to upgrade your questions so you can upgrade your answers to their needs and begin to separate yourself from the competition. Why is this new perspective critical to your success? Because, it's important to understand that the first answer they give you may not be the complete answer. It may not contain the real answer or ultimate reason for their greatest concern. The only way to discover the real answer is to keep asking probing questions in a respectful way that draws them into the process.

The sequence may look something like this:

Level 1 — Standard Question —> Standard Answer (SQ1 —> SA1)

Level 2 — Probing Question —> Cautious Answer (PQ2 —> CA2)

Level 3 — Probing Question —> Clearer Answer (PQ3 —> CA3)

Level 4 — Probing Question —> Real Answer (PQ4 —> RA4)

Let's look at an example.

Preparation question you ask yourself:

Standard Question – "What do they want?"

Upgrade Question – "What do they *really* want?"

Actual question you may ask your prospect or customer:

Standard Question – "How will this decision help your business?"

Upgrade Question – "In addition to solving this issue, is there any other reason this solution is important to you?"

The difference in the questions you ask can be the difference between your product or service being recognized as the best solution or just one of many.

What you're really looking for is the answer behind the answer. Probing questions start to take on a different vibe when you ask any of the following:

"Tell me why this is important to you."

"How will this impact your growth strategy in the next three to six months?"

"If you don't take action now, what other challenges may be ahead for you?"

"What other issues are of great concern for you in the upcoming year?"

"Do you have any additional plans for expansion?"

And so on ...

The Gift that Keeps on Giving

With each passing year, one thing is for certain—you are going to get new sales goals for the coming year. All my years of representative selling (B2B4C) have contained one consistent annual gift: ***New Year = New Goals!***

The company comes to you and tells you what production numbers you need to hit this year. I know for some this can be scary. In the previous year, if you have outperformed your territory goals by a wide margin, you will be asked to keep up the momentum and grow big again in the new year. This can heap a large amount of pressure on you to find a handful of large accounts you'll need to write to hit your new goals. This can cause you to lose sight of managing your time effectively. It's common for most salespeople to make their primary focus the uncovering of big opportunities if they hope to hit their numbers. In the sales world, this is often referred to as "elephant hunting!" You are constantly looking for the big target, the one or two large accounts, which will help you reach your new goals. I have seen this strategy from management handcuff excellent sales reps as they shift from what got them to where they are, to the pressure of staying on top.

If you fell short of your goals in the previous year, the focus on your process and hitting your numbers becomes more microscopic in measure. You're likely to have weekly and monthly reviews which are much more pointed in getting you to focus on closing more deals. This pressure can be overwhelming and if you are not led by your superior, but are micro-managed, you are not living in your sweet spot.

When the focus is overwhelmingly on your goals, you lose sight of the most important perspective—the ultimate customer and their needs.

Selling is Serving

Innovative ideas are an important part of the sales process. No one likes to keep doing the same things over and over again, especially when the results aren't there. Yes, perseverance is beneficial. Spinning your wheels is not. Keep your mind and energy fresh by thinking more about your customers than your process. It's a cart and horse thing. For those of you who don't relate to that analogy, think about how in certain cultures or past times, a horse-drawn cart was a common way to transport people or food or materials. To gain the benefit of the strength of the horse for the job, you would not put the cart before the horse. This would be out of order and ineffective in accomplishing what you really want. The sustaining strength of the horse comes from pulling the cart not pushing it. If you visited New York City, and were looking for a unique experience, you might consider hiring a horse-drawn carriage to ride around Central Park. Notice it's not called a carriage-drawn horse! That wouldn't make any sense. Neither is grinding after your goals with no sense or understanding of what your customer wants.

If you want to gain traction in accomplishing your sales goals, shift your mindset to focus on how you can best serve the needs of your customer. This strategy lifts the burden of hitting your sales goals or having the pressure to close the deal to win with your boss. Free yourself from the pressure of hitting your numbers and focus on meeting the needs of your customer.

Adjusting your focus away from your products or services (what) to your customer and their needs (who) will lead you to greater connection and opportunity to add value to others. As you approach each sales experience, recognize that every customer connection is an opportunity. One of the most significant shifts you can make in your sales perspective is to understand your purpose before you meet with your customer. In other words, change your thinking from *what* you're there for to *who* you're there for.

Let your mindset remain in the posture of serving your client and/or customer. Believe it or not, two things will happen:

1. They will take notice when your focus is on them and their needs and not your own!

2. You have put yourself in the best position to hit your numbers!

That is not a misprint. The second point above is real and you will be amazed that your numbers end up taking care of themselves when you stop dwelling on them. When you focus on the needs of your clients and customers, your numbers will be just fine. You may even find yourself consistently exceeding your goals. Remember, the real secret is, this isn't about numbers, it's about relationships!

The 86% Outcome Perspective

Let me share with you a perspective on how I was able to engage a high success rate for my clients and their customers by keeping the focus on the ultimate customer throughout the entire process.

2010-2012 – For three years I averaged an 86% success rate when I went out with an agent and presented the details of the Self-Insured Group that I represented. This was not a standard insurance program. The best results in sales came when the story was told properly to ensure that the prospect understood how this program was different from traditional insurance and delivered greater benefit to their bottom line. Clearly communicating the details of the program allowed the prospect to make the best decision for their business. My results for these three years were based on a range of 35 to 40 opportunities each year to present this program with my client to their prospects. This simply meant that my client/agent consistently wrote new business when I presented this program on their behalf.

2012-2024 – I went to work in the traditional insurance market where it wasn't required as often that I present with the agent to their prospect. My history of success did occasionally get me invited to join the agent (3-5 times/year) in presenting my company's solution to the specific needs of the prospect. As of this writing, the success rate for the agent when I present with them is 100%! That's right! In the last 12 years I have been undefeated in helping the agent write the business with my company when I was invited to join them in presenting the solutions to their customers!

I did not use any standard closing techniques that are common is sales. I chose to keep my focus on getting to the bottom of what was most important to the customer. Their perspective was paramount to me. Everything else was set aside. This was also a disarming strategy as I never arrived at a point in the conversation where I directly asked for the sale. Once they realized that I was there for them and not me, they would decide to move forward, and the sale would most often close itself. My intent here is not to brag. I simply want you to know that the method I developed years ago about effectively approaching every encounter with a prospect has worked! It required keeping the perspective of the customer as top priority in every decision I made and every sentence I uttered.

Words matter.

Value matters.

Communicating to the needs of the customer will put you in the best position to win!

Defining Value

Defining value is not your job! It's uncovering what your customer values that makes the difference! The best way to communicate value is to first find out how your prospect defines value! If you define value for them, then you are not serving their needs. Seek to understand your prospect by asking what's most important to them. Let them define value for themselves. When you help them uncover what they really value, they'll naturally let you in on it, as you process the answer together. Remember the sales process is about their story, not yours.

EXAMPLE: Prior to my insurance career, I used to design kitchens. It was common for a prospect to ask me for my opinion about a design choice. They would often say, "If this were your kitchen, what would you do?" My common response was to let them know that when this project was over, they would be the ones enjoying their new kitchen and not me. I would immediately go back over all the things I learned about what was important to them when we first met. You see, my early discussions with them were always about what options and features they wanted, and I got some initial feedback from them about their preferences for certain design features. As a result, when a decision needed to be made, I would refer to the preferences they had originally shared with me. This ensured they saw my focus was on what they wanted, not what I wanted.

It was vital to me that when this project was completed, they would say, "I'm glad we did …!" rather than, "I wish we would have …!"

Keeping the customer's perspective as the most important perspective in any sales experience delivers value well beyond the transaction. Every time a visitor would see their new kitchen, they would talk about the features with joy and enthusiasm, and naturally follow the conversation with a referral to me. I learned an important lesson and came to understand my winning strategy: Help them win first and eventually I'll win.

Once you understand the value definition is not yours to determine, you are on your way to helping your customers win. I encourage you to make this strategy your own personal mission.

> *Your winning strategy: Help them win first and eventually you'll win.*

The Takeaway

Walking away from a new business opportunity is one of the most challenging lessons to learn, especially when you are early in your career and hungry for business. I received a fitting example of what posturing looks like when I went out on a prospective visit with my boss, Stu Thompson, and one of our agents who set up the appointment. Stu invited me along to a couple of prospect meetings to get a glimpse of one of my potential roles with the company under his leadership. He wanted me to see how he and the agent presented our self-insured program to potential members.

When we entered the owner's office, after the initial greetings, the agent opened by confirming why we were there and what we would be sharing with him. From the outset, the owner gave no indication of either excitement or indifference. He listened as the agent handed the conversation over to Stu who would be discussing the self-insured workers' comp program.

Before launching into a sales talk on features and benefits of the program, Stu started by asking questions of the owner. His initial questions were designed to check the pulse of the owner on any issues he had with his current coverage. The owner became passive with his answers. Then Stu asked the owner if he'd be open to moving his business for the right opportunity. The owner's answer told the story. He paused and was vague in his reply. The owner indicated that he had heard a little about this program and he wasn't sure it was for him and that he was satisfied with his current coverage. As he articulated his position out loud and essentially confirmed he was not open to this new idea, Stu simply closed his notebook to indicate that any pressure the owner might be feeling was over. Stu asked a couple of additional questions and then shared a concluding statement letting the owner know if he ever changed his mind about reviewing an option that could benefit his business in the future to let us know. He stood up and thanked the man for his time.

As we walked out of that building and got into the car, Stu told us that there was no sense spending another minute in that office with someone who was unwilling to change. It was not about right or wrong, good, or bad, happy, or sad. It was simply acknowledging that this solution isn't for someone who is closed-minded. Stu went on to tell me that this program isn't for everyone. Not everyone can see it and there may be reasons why they don't tell us what's going on in their business. And he said that was okay. We just need to tell the story about our solution to people who are looking to solve a problem that our program can deliver for their business.

It's not every day you get to witness the power of walking out of a meeting. I learned that telling them everything is not the answer. It's about finding out if they have a problem they are looking to solve. If your product or service can help them, then share your potential solution. If your product or service does not meet their needs, then respect their time, and keep moving.

Try ABH Instead of ABC

What if your products or services don't offer a solution for their specific issues? Your confirming response may simply acknowledge you are unable to help them and conclude right there. Don't be bashful about the opportunity to bring clarity to your prospect even when you can't help them. They will appreciate you for your honesty and candor.

Out of courtesy, you may also offer them a recommendation or referral to another person or organization that has the potential to help them. Keeping your mindset focused on the most important perspective in every situation helps you recognize the times that being willing to help them find a solution elsewhere is still serving them. This appropriate strategy of always being helpful flies in the face of the traditional strategy of closing techniques.

If you've been involved in some area of sales, it's likely you have heard a reference to or even have seen the 1992 movie *Glengarry Glen Ross,* which depicts a two-day window into the lives of four real estate salesmen. They are confronted with the motivational trainer sent from home office to threaten them with the message that at the end of the promotional period for the new property development they represented, only the two top salesmen will keep their jobs, and the rest will be fired. After accusing them all of being losers, not possessing what it takes to close the real estate leads they've been given, the motivational trainer gives them a "pep-talk" where he impresses the importance of the *A-B-Cs* of sales: *Always Be Closing!* [11]

There is a certain unspoken pressure that appears when the standard time in a conversation turns to a decision. The customer is familiar with this part of the sales experience and typically goes to some type of defensive posture. The salesperson is also trained in this area to use multiple approaches to get their customer into a position to be closed. As if it's some sort of sales dance, both parties assume their positions and begin to move ...

Hold it! Stop trying to close the sale!

Chose instead to *Always Be Helpful!* Although A-B-H may not have the same ring to it as the A-B-Cs of sales, the building of your reputation in the marketplace is immeasurable. You'd be surprised how often your prospect comes back to you for another opportunity to help them or refer you to a friend of theirs when your posture is all about helping them. They remember the type of people they want to do business with. Find ways to serve your prospects and customers, even if you end up referring them on to someone else, and you will be blessed in the long run.

Pressuring someone or serving someone—both strategies have an impact on your reputation. Ask yourself how you want to be known in the marketplace. Everything you do and say builds your character and your reputation.

Your New Game Plan

One of the most effective things you can do to grow your business is to be curious! It's not a secret, although it is often missed as an important strategy in successfully serving others. I will also confirm to your that curiosity fuels your enthusiasm! Your attitude and curiosity for what your customer thinks and what they are looking to solve will help you engage the proper strategy to help them get what they want. Your job is not to sell them anything. Keep the plan simple for both you and your prospect. Find out what they want. If it's within your ability, give them access to it. You'd be surprised how many people will thank you for helping them gain access to what they want as a solution to their problem.

Over the years I've had customers come to me because of the solutions I've provided to their friends and even their competitors. The reputation you leave is important. When you strive to be a problem-solver, people will seek you out because they recognize your value.

Sales Perspective Habits

Start
- Eliminate closing from your vocabulary and your strategy.

Analyze
- Look for opportunities to think bigger regarding how you can add value to your customers.

Learn
- Be willing to consider a variety of ways to be helpful.
- Let your curiosity guide you to new possibilities for your customer.

Engage
- Be open to new ideas and be willing to take positive action toward serving your customers.

Serve
- It's time to realize that selling is serving. Give your best to your prospects and customers every day!

PART TWO
THE BRIDGE

5
THE ESSENTIAL SELLING PERSPECTIVE (ESP) METHOD

FEATURING THE FIVE CS OF EVERY SALES EXPERIENCE — YOUR NEW GAME PLAN FOR SUCCESS

> *"Four steps to achievement: Plan purposefully. Prepare prayerfully. Proceed positively. Pursue persistently."* [12]
> — William A. Ward

Diffusing the Bear

I WAS ASKED TO do a sales presentation for the first time with Matt, a new agent, selling our workers' comp program and trying to win the business of this prospective customer. We met at the prospect's office and as we entered the building the agent told me that I would kick off the presentation. Because I was representing only one of the lines of business he would be sharing that day, he asked me to leave when I completed my part so he could finish the balance of his entire package presentation. As we waited in the office area, we were notified that the owner was out in the warehouse and would be in momentarily. This was a new prospective customer for Matt, who was invited in see if he could earn this company's insurance business. So we were both going to be building relationship bridges. My strategy was to accomplish my part by properly edifying this agent to the owner, uncover the solutions he was looking for, and to look for opportunities to deliver value, service, and trust with this prospect.

Suddenly, the owner appeared! He was a big, broad-shouldered man with a commanding presence. He approached us and said, "Thanks for waiting." After the introductions, he invited us all to go to the lower-level conference room. He took two steps and then stopped in his tracks, raised his index finger, and said, "I just want to warn you, the shorter this is the better your chances are with me today. Follow me." What an opening! As he escorted us down the stairs to the break room where we would be meeting, I thought to myself, *"How am I going to diffuse the bear?"* After all, I was going first!

My presentations to prospects typically lasted anywhere from 20 to 30 minutes, depending on the number of questions they asked. So, there I was, walking down the hallway toward our destination, and I knew that I needed to change my strategy and tighten things up a bit. OK, a lot!

As we sat down on the opposite side of the table from the "bear" he sat with his arms crossed, leaned back in his chair, and looked at us to get this meeting going. The agent thanked him for his willingness to meet with us and promised to move efficiently through the entire presentation to honor his time. To make sure that he had a good understanding of the program the agency was proposing to him, the agent introduced me as a representative from the insurance company to describe the details of the workers' compensation part of the package. The bear looked intently at me.

Knowing that time was of the essence I asked him a clarifying question to try and uncover what was most important to him. As I started to ask him another question based upon his first answer, he pushed my question aside and said, "I just want you to know, I've seen this before. I saw this program when you were just getting started. Some of my buddies joined way back in the beginning. I didn't think that you were going to get enough companies to buy-in to your concept." His response let me know that his understanding of my company and how our program worked was inaccurate or incomplete. Rather than spend time correcting him, I focused on clarifying how the primary details of this program would specifically answer his greatest concerns with his current insurance coverage. Being prepared helped me to listen attentively to his responses to my initial questions and quickly identify his concerns. I responded with the specific solutions our program would bring to his business. As I engaged him with questions, he slowly uncrossed his arms and leaned in to make sure that he understood the key advantages in our program. He began asking me clarifying questions and was no longer in a defensive posture. I recognized he was gaining interest in how this workers' comp program would directly benefit his business.

I wrapped up and asked him if he had any further questions before I left. He told me no, and paying attention to the importance of time, I stood up to leave, leaned toward him and closed with one last statement. I said, "Matt thought enough of you to invite me here today to make sure you have enough of the right information about how this program works so you can make the best decision for your business. It may not have been right for you when our concept was new, but I am pleased to let you know there are over eight hundred members, including some of your friends, already taking advantage of the benefits of this program. Now is the time to ask yourself if these advantages outweigh what you're getting with your current program. Let me know if any additional questions come up. You can reach me directly or contact Matt about this workers' comp program." I let that linger for just a moment.

He stood up to look me in the eye, shook my hand, and thanked me for taking the time to come out to his office and properly explain this opportunity to him. I thanked him for his time and said my good-byes to him and Matt and got out of there.

I reached my car, looked at my watch, and realized that I had just presented my program to his satisfaction in 12 minutes! I went to a nearby coffee shop to wait to hear from my agent about his impressions on how he thought everything went. Less than 30 minutes later, he called to say that he finished presenting the rest of the insurance package and was amazed and kind of dumbfounded that this "bear" transformed before his eyes and became receptive, almost enthusiastic, about the entire presentation.

Matt said to me, "How did you do that?" I explained that I realized from his prospect's opening statement that going straight to features and benefits would not effectively accomplish anything for this busy business owner. I had to uncover his greatest need first and then present the details of my program in the form of solutions that met his needs. The agent asked me if I would help train him to understand the program better so he, too, could move beyond features and benefits alone. I told him it would be my pleasure, and we made an appointment to follow up with more training.

Matt told me the incumbent agent was presenting later in the day and the owner would call him by the end of the day with his decision. I asked him to let me know if any other questions came up and that I looked forward to hearing from him with the outcome of the decision.

My phone rang at 5:30pm with the words, "We have a new customer! We were awarded all of his business." Matt thanked me for my help and said I was instrumental in helping the owner make his decision. The owner told Matt that he gave him the business because he placed enough value on his business to invite me to the appointment to make sure he understood how the program really works. "Thanks again," Matt said. "I will see you next week when we meet for training. Great job today!"

"Congratulations, Matt, on doing your homework in securing this new account," I replied. I told him it was my pleasure to help him and was looking forward to doing this again soon.

A Quick Review

My initial observation around this story is that reading your prospect is critical to your connection. Thinking that simply pounding out features and benefits to a prospective customer without finding out what they really need will miss the mark most of the time. Remember, it's not about us; it's about the customer. To deliver value, service, and trust, I had to uncover and engage all three throughout the meeting. Learning about his business and industry in advance allowed me to receive his initial objections and turn them into specific questions, strategies, and solutions relatable to his unique situation. His posture changed as I sought to understand where he was coming from and found ways to help him see how this solution could benefit his business in ways he didn't initially understand.

Lessons Learned – A New Mindset

This big win caused me to reflect on the entire process. I wanted to understand and evaluate all aspects of this sale so I could determine how to duplicate this experience and provide a repeatable strategy to bring about consistent results in delivering value to my clients and customers. I saw several takeaways when I stopped to review why my chosen strategy worked.

Here are the key lessons that can be learned from this experience:

- Put others first (get your focus off yourself and keep it on your prospect)

- Clarity attracts – confusion repels (the simpler the message the better)

- Don't say everything; say the *right* thing (use language that fits this customer)

- Leave before they are ready for you to leave (honor their time – don't hang around)

As I examined each of these lessons, one thing that stood out for me was my internal battle to tell him everything I knew about my products and services. It's a common problem in sales. Most sales professionals have the features and benefits drilled into them before they ever present to a prospect. One way that helps me keep my mind focused on what's most important to my prospect before I meet with them is continually repeating this statement to myself before I ever set foot in front of them:

"What I have to say is not as important as what they need to hear!"

Keep this perspective alive in your mind before, during, and after every meeting and you will show your prospect or customer that you are there to help them! I love how the fundamental technique from Dale Carnegie, that was shared back in chapter two, points directly to the heart of this perspective. Carnegie says, "So the only way on earth to influence other people is to talk about what they want and show them how to get it." [13]

When you take your eyes off yourself and put them on the other person, you'll learn to set your mind on their needs and thus position yourself to deliver a solution that can meet or even exceed their expectations.

Sales Goals

Before getting into the new framework and process that will transform your business, let's look at some of the additional factors that can muddle your thinking when you prepare to engage your prospects and customers.

No matter the industry or type of sales you are engaged in, there are always goals that come with the territory. Goals are usually formulated by answering the following questions:

- What has happened? (Past)

- What is happening? (Present)

- What needs to happen? (Future)

Each year in my sales career I am given goals to accomplish in the year ahead. They are typically based upon trends and other factors in the marketplace and include our company strategy for growth and market share in the coming year. These strategies are designed to help the organization address the budget and growth initiatives that feed the bottom line.

My company's strategies are important, but I never let these goals rule my daily thinking. While I am responsible for the accomplishment of those goals to help the company meet its objectives and help me keep my job, I have never let them distract me from helping my client win with their customer.

Your New Game Plan for Success

"Forget about goals and focus on systems." When I read this statement by author James Clear my mind immediately resonated with the words and I said to myself, *"Yes, that's exactly right!"* Now, before we get carried away and lose sight of the purpose of this fundamental message, let's put this statement into proper context.

In his book, *Atomic Habits*, Clear lays out a simple game plan for understanding the difference between goal-setting versus systems. "Goals are about the results you want to achieve. Systems are about the processes that lead to those results," says Clear. He continues, "Goals are good for setting a direction, but systems are best for making progress." [14]

The reason I was so excited about this thinking when I first read it, is I have found lasting success in selling over my career using this strategy. Having a framework that identifies the big picture (goal) which is supported by the process (system) delivers consistent results over time.

Introducing The Essential Selling Perspective (ESP) Method

Time and experience have taught me there is a perspective in sales that is often overlooked and underappreciated. I call it the Essential Selling Perspective (ESP) Method. This is the framework that changed everything for me. This is where my focus changed from what I wanted and what I assumed my customer wanted to learning about what my customer *really* wanted. This newfound perspective will be the difference-maker in your sales results. Once I started giving my customers what they really wanted, my numbers took care of themselves. Let me say that again:

"Once I started giving my customers what they really wanted, my numbers took care of themselves."

These three factors are the heart of what the customer wants in a sales experience. Stop trying to close the sale! Engage your Essential Selling Perspective (ESP) and start giving your customers what they want most:

Value – Service – Trust

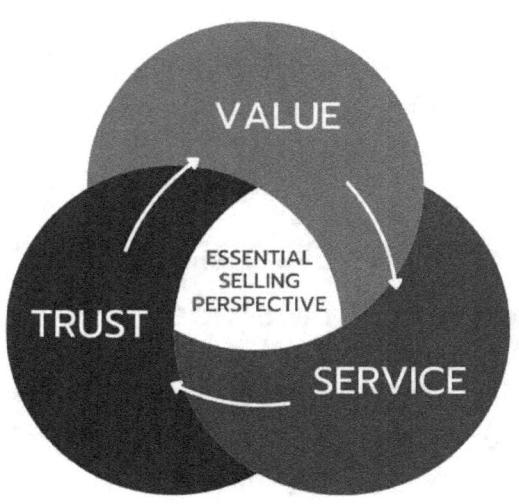

Because it is imperative to see things from the customer's perspective, let's look at some standard definitions for clues as to how to apply these definitions to the sales methodology.

Value: 1) the monetary worth of something; (market price). 2) a fair return or equivalent in goods, services, or money for something exchanged. 3) to consider or rate highly; (prize or esteem). 4) to rate or scale in usefulness, importance, or general worth; (evaluate).

Service: 1) the work performed by one that serves; (help, use, benefit). 2) contribution to the welfare of others.

Trust: 1) assured reliance on the character, ability, strength, or truth of someone or something. 2) one in which confidence is placed. 3) to place confidence in; (rely on). 4) to hope or expect confidently. [13]

When it comes to sales, we can get more specific as we apply these definitions. I've found that there are three specific facets that apply to each factor. When you look at each factor in the following manner, everything opens up for you and for the customer.

The three facets are:

1. The Person

2. The Business

3. The Problem

Essential Selling Perspective Method

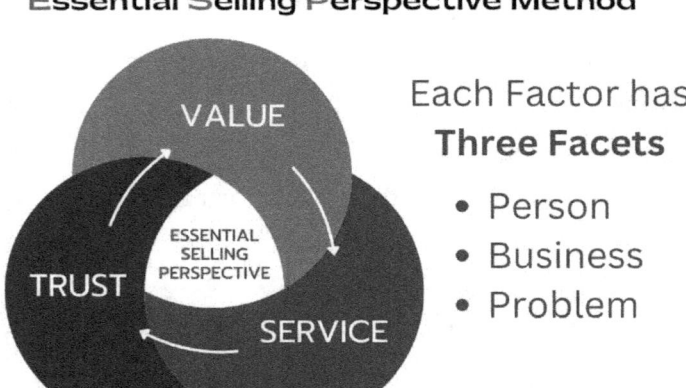

When determining how to add **Value** to your customer, start with valuing the owner of the business you are calling on, value the business they are in, and value the problem they are trying to solve. When you are that specific with the value you add to your customer, they will recognize that you are there for them. This alone will separate you from the majority of your competition!

Apply the same to **Service** by serving the customer, serve their business and their employees, and serve the people responsible for implementing the solution. For **Trust**, keep the owner informed throughout the entire process, empower the employees, and praise them to the owner when appropriate, and follow up and follow through with those who implement the solution, making sure they are satisfied with the result.

When these three facets are consistently applied to each factor in the Essential Selling Perspective, and you close the loop in

Value, Service, and Trust, it can lead to additional business or even referrals to additional prospects known by the business owner.

Take the time to remember the importance of each facet and how it applies to each factor:

- *Value* the person, the business, and the problem they are trying to solve.
    - Your connection with all facets is critical.
- *Service* the person, the business and their employees, and the team who will implement the solution.
    - Communication is key.
- *Trust* the person, the business, and the entire organization, and follow through with the team that delivered them to a "post-problem" operating status.
    - Deliver a deeper bond beyond the transaction.

You may think that closing the deal trumps all the strategies in the world and this belief reveals where your focus lies. Remember, this is not about you! I realize this may be a stretch for some of you as your "closer" instincts want to kick in. No worries. I used to be in the same place. However, there is nothing like getting beaten up in the marketplace to refine your perspective about what's most valued by your prospects. Save yourself time and energy by plugging into this method and its proven track record. When I keep my mind clear about serving the needs of my prospects and customers, my sales goals take care of themselves every year.

Delivering the highest impact for your customers is built on the framework of the ESP Method. Knowing what they want and what's most important to your customer helps you discern if the product or service you offer provides the solution they are looking for in their business.

Why is employing a method for your sales process important? Every sales opportunity has its own unique characteristics; however, "winging it" in your sales approach often leads to a disconnect with your prospect. When you are disconnected, they won't trust you or feel confident enough to see your value in delivering a solution for them. Don't leave your success to chance. Put a method in place that consistently works and is dependable in delivering value, service, and trust.

Your framework deserves your best effort because your prospect deserves your best effort, and your career deserves your best effort. Following a method (a way, technique, or process of or for doing something), takes the guesswork out of the things you can control. This will set your mind at ease and give you a way to measure your success and failure. No one makes every single sale and there will be times that your prospect decides to go with someone else, postpone their decision to move forward, or wait altogether. But using the ESP Method will get you closer to the target each time.

The System That Makes Your Framework Work

When a sales professional is given their goals for the year, it's common to think, "OK. Now that I know where I'm going, how do I get there?" If that's you, I have a solution for you: the *Five Cs of Every Sales Experience* – The keys to the ESP Method framework.

The *Five C's of Every Sales Experience* is where you'll learn the value of having the framework for your goals and the system designed to help you accomplish those goals. Through this game plan (framework and process), you will step into a world where you will:

- Stand out from the competition

- Achieve high-impact results for your customer and your company

- Turn your prosects into life-long relationships

- Establish a reputation that gets you invited back again and again

This is not trivial. If you are looking for a strategy that works and keeps on working, read on. I will share real-world examples of situations I have learned from, navigated through, and overcome. This proven framework and process will provide a stress-free sales strategy so you can keep your focus on your prospect or customer.

Once I implemented this game plan consistently, my results were transformed. My colleagues started asking me what I was doing to increase my impact and drive consistent results.

I have been in a representative selling role for over two decades. In that time, I've learned the consistency with which you treat people will always get you invited back into their office, their business opportunities, and their lives. Most of my clients would say they want to do business with people they know and who see them on a regular basis. When it comes to delivering the kind of value that opens the door to your customer's head and heart, understand that it's not about how many deals you close. It starts with you bringing value to the relationship.

When working directly with a customer, I've always tried to help them by understanding their problem and then bringing the solution that addresses their biggest needs. When I work in a representative sales situation with my client, who sells my products to their customer, I focus on helping my client win with their customer. Either way, it's always about the customer.

My greatest discovery was learning how to accomplish the goals bestowed upon me each year by placing my focus on my client's or customer's needs. I began to make a consistent effort to relate to them and serve their needs. To make sure my goals would take care of themselves, rather than focusing on closing deals, I employed a consistent process that I call the *Five Cs of Every Sales Experience*.

Five Cs of Every Sales Experience

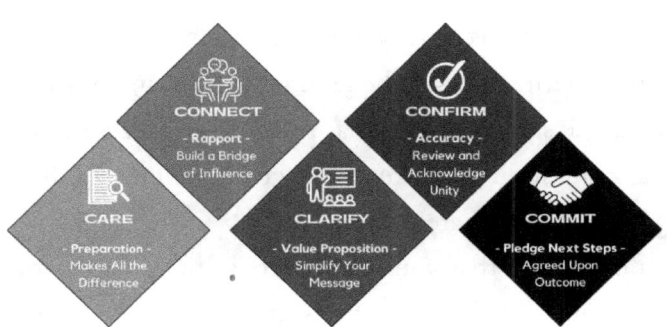

These five steps in the sales process: **Care – Connect – Clarify – Confirm – Commit**, have brought me decades of success in building relationships and earning my clients business. This is a sequenced process that works consistently in building relationships that turn into a long-term business strategy. It has been proven over decades of application.

Why 'Sales Experience?'

Because we're not talking about closing strategies here, the focus will be on the sales *experience* your customer has with you. How you work with them and for them shows how you value them in the sales process. It's not about positioning them for the close, it's about making sure they have an amazing experience when dealing with you.

According to my good friend Joe Pine and his co-author Jim Gilmore, in their best-selling book *The Experience Economy*, they provide a specific look at the importance of experiences. "Experiences have necessarily emerged to create new value. Such experience offerings occur whenever a company intentionally uses services as the stage and goods as props to engage an individual. Whereas commodities are fungible, goods tangible, and services intangible, *experiences* are memorable." [14]

It's no surprise that your customers want an experience that shows they are valued over the transaction. They don't want to be sold. They want to be valued and participate in the experience with you. When you make the experience about them, they can't help but feel that your focus is on what they want. This step ensures that they don't feel sold or manipulated. It also helps them to avoid any feelings of buyer's remorse. All these elements make the experience a positive one and lead to referral opportunities. It's amazing how treating someone well gives them confidence to share your name with someone else who can also benefit from what you have to offer, especially when what you have to offer is a valuable experience!

Remember that this is your opportunity to set yourself apart from your competition. Is it true that most people like to do business with people they like and can relate to? Yes! Make every effort to be that person by making intentional connections and increasing the value of the sales experience. People end up feeling they weren't sold when they were supported to make the best decision for their business. Now that's a great sales experience!

New Sales Shift – When the Sale Really Happens

If you are interested in the myriad of closing strategies, know that they are written about and shared in a variety of forms designed to deliver the greatest results. Of course, the results are most often measured in close rates and not necessarily in value provided. Pressures that are paired with your sales goals often drive sales professionals to focus too much on hitting your goals and not enough on serving your clients or customers.

I scheduled a meeting with Dustin Swenson, one of my clients and a producer with Nesbit Agencies, Minnetonka, Minnesota, to discuss new business opportunities. I've had the privilege of knowing Dustin for over 18 years and have watched him grow his business by making customer relationships his top priority. I asked him about his sales strategy and how he proceeds through the sales process and keeps the needs of the customer paramount. I shared my Five Cs approach and then asked him if he uses any closing techniques. He told me he hasn't used any specific closing techniques in a long time. He smiled and said, "Once I realized the sale closed itself in the middle of the process, everything changed." This acknowledgement is so important I want you to read it again!

> **"Once I realized the sale closed itself in the middle of the process, everything changed."**

Dustin went on to tell me that he follows a specific process for building the relationship with his prospect's organization, and if he stays true to the process, the sale gets confirmed along the way. He hasn't had to resort to any closing strategies at the end of the process. When he develops the appropriate relationship by showing his prospect that their needs are his primary focus, they end up wanting to do business with him, without requiring the specific ask at the end of the process.

The strong trust relationship I have built with Dustin over the years has only increased my level of respect and admiration for who he is and the way he does business.

In the coming chapters I will walk you through the details of each of the Five Cs and I want you to notice something specific: Even though this is a book about sales strategies, *closing* is not one of the Cs. What would you say if I told you I could show you how to close more deals without focusing on a variety of closing strategies? Well, that's exactly what this method can bring to you. As a sales professional, you are on the road to gaining clarity and focus on what's most important to growing your business. You are about to discover how to address each of these steps in sequence and develop the benefits that get you invited back time after time.

Sales Perspective Habits

Start
- Set your mind on what matters most in the eyes of your customer.

Analyze
- Dig into the details of the ESP Method.
- Develop an understanding of Value, Service, and Trust and pursue the answers to them in every sales experience.

Learn
- Get to know the fundamentals of the process, the Five Cs of Every Sales Experience, and learn how to make them work for you.

Engage
- Trust the steps and then customize them to your personality, products, and services.

Serve
- Let your customer decide along the way if your value fits their need.
- Keep the focus on their solution

CARE

PREPARATION MAKES ALL THE DIFFERENCE

"People don't care how much you know until they know how much you care." [15]

— attributed to Theodore Roosevelt

A Welcome Word

I ONCE RECEIVED A call from someone who said to me, "I've been thinking about you. I just wanted to reach out and see how you're doing." As you may imagine, this lifted my spirits immediately. It was a welcome word to know that someone was spending time thinking about me! In a world where self-focus seems to be a common theme, when you take the opportunity to care more about your customer than yourself, you'll separate yourself from the majority of your competition.

Get Started Right

Making great connections and having a powerful impact on your clients and customers starts long before you meet. The time you spend learning what's most important to the customer is never wasted. It will make all the difference in helping you connect in ways that your competition won't! You may initially think it's not that important, but I encourage you to reconsider. Think of this strategy as the key investment you make in getting to know your prospects before you meet them.

In my early days of selling, I was less concerned about doing all the extra homework prior to meeting with a client or customer. I'd try to size them up on the spot and go from there. I thought *winging it* was an appropriate strategy, and it took me some time to figure out that my ability to make a strong connection with a prospect starts before we meet. I've learned through experience there is great wisdom and truth in the following statement by Benjamin Franklin:

> **"By failing to prepare, you are preparing to fail."** [16]

What surprised me was the more I prepared in advance of a meeting, the better prepared I was to pivot during the meeting. We can walk into meetings all set with our plan and agenda, yet time and again, your prospect may have something else altogether planned to get the meeting started. Your ability to pivot and not get thrown off by the urgency of what someone else wants to deal with is built into your preparation time. In other words, if you are well prepared for what you want to cover, you will be better positioned to serve your client or customer, even when they want to start the meeting with their priorities first, or something new that's urgent to them.

Preparation

A quote by Stephen Keague, author of *The Little Red Handbook of Public Speaking and Presenting*, sums up the importance of being prepared for your best presentation to your client or customer.

> **"Proper planning and preparation prevents poor performance."** [17]

Imagine walking into a meeting, and after your initial introductions and before the meeting gets started, your customer asks for your advice about a specific question on their mind not related to what you expected to talk about. How do you manage the situation? What is your response?

- Do you address their question with a general answer?

- Do you defer your answer to a later time in your presentation where you will address the topic?

- Do you ask clarifying questions to make sure you understand what they're asking?

- Do you tell them exactly how they should handle it?

- Do you ask permission to do additional investigation or give their question more thought and promise to follow up with them at a future date?

This situation is more commonplace in sales than most sales professionals care to admit. However, when your focus is on helping your client have a positive impact on their customer, you can build the kind of trust that shows them that you care about their business.

A Revealing Question

In the spring of 2022, I did a live, online presentation to a group of insurance agents. As a result of that presentation, an agency owner that I knew from my past reached out to me. He had changed careers and bought an agency along with a partner in central Minnesota. I agreed to visit their agency and share with them how my products and services could help them grow their business.

I walked into the office of Insurance Leaders Agency, LLC, in Hutchinson, Minnesota, and met with new owners Bryan Eastep and Chad Carlson. I knew Bryan from the years when our families were growing up and we attended the same church in the Twin Cities. I was meeting Chad for the first time, and it was fun to connect and get to know more about how these two met and subsequently made the decision to shift their careers and buy this agency. I asked questions and let them tell me their story. (FYI – everyone loves to tell their origin story. Don't ever shy away from this important glimpse into the motivations that owners had and still have for what they do and why they do it.) This conversation helped me ask better questions when we shifted to how my products and services line up with their vision. Because my company and our products and services were new to this agency, I spent some time talking to them about how we are positioned to be a strong agency partner for their customers, which in turn would help them grow.

They asked great questions throughout our discussion. Chad seemed especially curious, and I soon found out why. As we wrapped up our primary conversation, he leaned forward, paused, and then asked permission to take our conversation in a different direction. He said, "Jimmy, I'm wondering if I could ask for your perspective on prospecting?" I replied, "Of course. What would you like to know?" He then proceeded to tell me about a new class of business he wanted to pursue and was looking for ideas about how to approach the owners of these local businesses. He said,

"Do you have any suggestions on the best ways to prospect these companies?"

I acknowledged his question and proceeded to tell him how important a good connection is when prospecting new customers. But I pointed out that it's not the first step!

I went on to explain the first step in prospecting is to care about their business. This caught his attention, and he wanted to know what I meant by "care about their business."

I suggested he start by learning as much as he can about their industry. Spend time looking into what the primary coverage needs are for this type of business and try to uncover if there are any opportunities to address, including something that others aren't asking them about. Answers to these questions can be a difference-maker for their business. There are a lot of details that can be learned about an industry through the state Department of Labor and Industry website. You can find out about issues and trends that impact their business.

I told him, "If you care enough about their business before you ever contact them, you will be able to ask better questions and demonstrate your concern for them by understanding the issues and opportunities they face every day."

To Care or Not to Care – That is the Question

Your first step in becoming a trusted advisor is to understand your prospect's industry and business needs. When this is done correctly before you ever meet them, you increase the chance of making a strong first impression. This strategy sets you apart from your competition and ensures you make an essential connection in your first meeting.

Remember, the more you familiarize yourself with their business, the more specific your questions will be. When you ask questions specific to their situation, they will start to realize that you care about their business.

This is your game-changer.

This will cause them to look at you as someone who has already invested the time to care about them and their business.

This is where partnerships are built.

When you start by giving them your best effort to understand their business *before you ever meet them*, it will help you treat them like a person and a business professional, and not like a transaction. This strategy puts you on a path that leads to a relationship where they will think of you as a trusted advisor. More specifically, as *their* trusted advisor!

The more you treat this process like a relationship and the less you treat it like a transaction, the greater connection you will ultimately make. Care enough about them and their business and allow them time to get to know who you are and how you can help them. When they know you care about them and their business, they will listen to your solutions and take you seriously.

Is It Worth It?

When trying to do all the groundwork in advance of reaching out to connect with a prospect, at some point along the way you're likely to ask yourself this question, "Is it worth it?" It's a fair question as you examine whether you are wasting your time with busy work or making worthwhile progress. All the prep work you do in advance of meeting your prospect increases the probability that you'll be able to make an authentic connection.

Most people in sales are striving to get in front of prospects to tell their story in hopes of making a sale. Your focus should be first on learning your prospect's story. You'd be amazed at what a difference this makes.

Robert Cialdini addresses how to put yourself in the best position win your customer over to your way of thinking through influence and persuasion. In his book, *PRE-SUASION*, he emphasizes the importance of the work you do before you ever meet with your prospect. He says, "The highest achievers spent more time crafting what they did and said *before* making a request. They set about their mission as skilled gardeners who know that even the finest seeds will not take root in stony soil or bear fruit in poorly prepared ground. They spent much of their time toiling in the fields of influence thinking about and engaging in cultivation—in ensuring that the situations they were facing had been pretreated and readied for growth."[18] A unique reminder of why doing proper prep work is vital to your success with a prospect. Don't delay this strategy and put it off for another time. You can't do it on the spot or on the fly. Put yourself in the best position to stand out from your competition and win the hearts of your prospects by caring about them before you ever meet with them.

Being Welcome Anywhere Starts Here

In Chapter 10, we'll discuss how to be welcome anywhere you go. It is ultimately the result of how you treat others, and it begins right here! Who doesn't want to be welcomed each time you connect with your customers? When you focus on the importance of gaining specific knowledge about your prospects and customers, you'll have the opportunity to build a relationship beyond business, which is a sweet result of simply caring about your customer.

I have good news for you: You can make sure you are welcomed anywhere you go by committing to make a difference every time you connect. What you are about to see is a pattern that has worked amazingly well for me and many other successful sales professionals over the years.

Please note that every sales experience is different primarily because you are dealing with the individual needs of the people you see. Day in and day out, these needs change. This doesn't mean you shouldn't have a plan. In fact, this should put greater emphasis on the importance of having a plan in place with the flexibility to move as your clients and customers want to move.

Laying the Groundwork

Many years ago, I walked into a meeting with one of my clients to present to his prospect the Workers' Comp program I represented. As we entered the owners office, before the agent had time to introduce me, the owner jumped up and said, "Oh my gosh,

Jimmy Z! It's so great to see you. We have all been wondering what happened to you as we haven't seen you teaching continuing education classes. You helped me get my contractor's license ten years ago!"

The agent looked at me and wondered what was going on. He observed the immediate and deep connection I had built years ago with his prospect. Of course, it was fun for me to celebrate with this owner on his success in business. We chatted about his origin story and how he has grown as a business owner. He was genuinely happy to see me and told me I had an impact on his launch by helping him successfully pass his licensing exam years ago when I was an insurance and contractor licensing trainer.

What struck me most about that meeting was learning how my delivering value through education when he was just getting started carried over into this chance meeting a decade later. The prior experience prepared him to expect something of value for his business now. As our conversation turned to the reason we were there, he listened with great interest, asked good questions, and made a decision on the spot to work with this agent. The solutions we presented to him were wrapped in the understanding of the value, service, and trust that were instilled in him years before. He knew from the value I once delivered to him, that he could easily trust me to do the same for him again.

When you take the time to care about someone else, the value you leave with them can last a lifetime.

Sales Perspective Habits

Start
- Start the process of getting to know your customer, their business, and the most common problems they might face before you ever meet them.

Analyze
- Do your homework and review the information to make sure you're not missing any important issues.

Learn
- Study the preparation tactics of other professions and industries to learn any best practices that you'll be able to duplicate regularly.

Engage
- Ask specific questions about your prospect, their business, and their biggest needs.

Serve
- Prepare your heart and mind to deliver value throughout the process of engaging.

Connect

RAPPORT — BUILD A BRIDGE OF INFLUENCE

"Try not to become a man of success. Rather become a man of value." [19]

— Albert Einstein

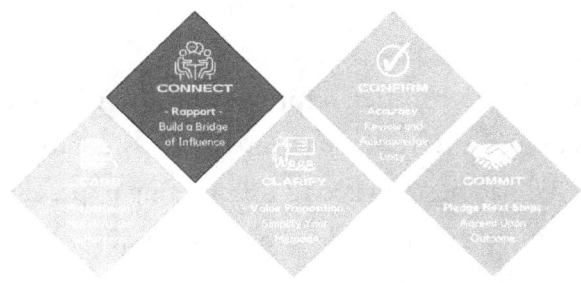

Let Their Stories Guide You

I HAD KNOWN OF Scherer Bros. Lumber for many years as several of my old customers from my days in the building supply industry had used them as their primary supplier for lumber, windows, and other products for the homes they built. On this day, I was invited by Tom Metzger, from Northern Capital Insurance, to meet him at the Scherer Bros. corporate office in Brooklyn Park, Minnesota. As we were escorted into the conference room off the main lobby, we were told the owners would be in shortly. Rather than sitting at the large table, I set my portfolio down and was immediately captivated by the pictures on the wall featuring the generations that told the story of this company that started in 1930. I liked their motto, "Same Commitment. Same Values. Same Family. Since 1930." I read the captions under each picture and learned so much about a family history that was clearly an integral part of the fabric of this organization. They were proud to tell their story, and they should be! A multi-generational, independent lumber company is a great success story.

As two of the brothers representing the third-generation owners entered the room, I immediately smiled as we were introduced. I had been invited to this meeting to present how my workers' comp program could provide a unique set of solutions to their organization. Yet before we began any discussion about my company, I started asking them about their business and its impressive history. I commented on how the pictures on display around the room told an amazing story and I wanted to know more. I asked them questions and they spoke with pride about their family history. After nearly fifteen minutes, I divulged that my interest was genuine as I, too, had grown up as the third generation in a family business prior to my current position in the insurance industry. With all sincerity, I conveyed my joy in seeing multi-generational family businesses succeed.

Expressing my joy at their story and their success opened the door for them to listen with interest as I shared the portions of our workers' comp program's story that addressed their specific needs. It also prompted them to ask very specific questions since they knew that I would have a greater understanding of what they needed, and the importance of which solutions were essential to their business. As our time came to a close (always be aware of the time you asked for and stick to it!), I stated that my goal was to help them make the best decision for their business. When I asked if they had any other questions, they said that we had covered everything to their satisfaction for today, and they would talk with Tom about the other lines of coverage they needed and get back to me with any additional questions. I thanked them, said our goodbyes, and established appropriate follow-up steps.

I walked out of that meeting with a connection that was genuine and appropriate for this business. By focusing on *their* story, it gave me the ability to relate specifically to their business and the potential solutions my product provided them. This approach would, by some sales standards, not have been direct enough or pressed in on getting them to decide on the spot, yet I read them appropriately by focusing on their story. You'd be amazed how many people like to tell their own story!

After all their questions were answered, Tom called me to tell me they would be moving forward with our program. He stated that they appreciated the details I shared to help them understand how our program would deliver specific value and address the issues for which they were seeking solutions.

How Stories Connect

In the story above, we see that focusing on the customer's story was an effective way to make a connection. I have seen others try to tell their own story hoping that along the way some part of their story finds a connection to their prospect. In my experience this my-story-first strategy is a huge gamble. Most people aren't interested in your story unless it provides a solution for their needs. How can you possibly know what they need if you never ask them, or you treat their story like an afterthought?

Don't leave them out. Don't fall prey to beating your own chest about how important you are, and your product is. They don't care until they know if it solves a problem for *them*. If you jump into your story first, you'll lose them before you can make any significant connection.

Make their story the only story that matters in the conversation. This posture helps to increase your connection to what they value most. Remember, the most important perspective belongs to the customer. Invite them into the conversation with curiosity about their story and pay attention to any parts of their story that overlap the products or services you have to offer.

Establish a Connection Right Away *and* the Right Way.

Your first contact is where you begin building a relationship. Rapport is the most common term ascribed to making an initial connection in sales, especially when you are meeting your client or customer for the first time. Rapport is defined as *a friendly, harmonious relationship; especially a relationship characterized by agreement, mutual understanding or empathy that makes communication possible or easy.* [20]

Many sales training frameworks talk about the importance of building rapport with a new or existing client at the front end of every meeting because this is a standard part of "best practices" and should be covered first before you can get down to your business agenda of the day.

I believe that rapport is more specific than that. Making a true connection requires preparation, attention to details, observing your surroundings, asking specific questions about their business, personal interests, family, charitable work, etc. Once you begin engaging by asking questions you must also do something that most people in sales simply will not do—listen with the intent to understand. Let me say that again. You should make an agreement with yourself that when you ask questions, you will stop everything else going on in your mind and *listen with the intent to understand!* This is also commonly referred to as *active listening.* I want you to excel at active listening!

Most people ask questions and then listen in the background of their mind as they are thinking of what they are going to say next, rather than truly listening to understand their clients as they respond to the question that was asked. Stephen R. Covey says, "Most people do not listen with the intent to understand; they listen with the intent to reply." [21]

Don't miss this! The very act of listening with the intent to understand, could be the difference in making a true connection with your client instead of just visiting with them and moving through some form of pleasant conversation so you can get to where you want the meeting to go. When your focus is on yourself and your needs, you miss out on making a true connection with your client.

NEWSFLASH!

Your client can tell when you are more interested in what your needs are than in what their needs are. They can assess rather quickly whether you are bringing them a solution that addresses their needs or simply focusing on your own needs. Remember, as you are sizing them up, they are sizing you up!

Are you a problem-solver?

Are you there for them or for yourself?

Are you trying to help their business or are you there to hit your sales goals?

When you don't make a proper connection, the rest of the meeting will fall flat in their mind, and you may not even know it!

Another effective way to make a connection is to disarm yourself in front of your client. I have found over the years that when I make fun of my own last name it puts everyone at ease.

They even start to ask questions about how to pronounce it, what it means, and why they like the nickname, "Jimmy Z," which helps them remember me when I call on them again. By having no fear about making fun of my own name and using it humorously as an icebreaker, it's amazing how many pretenses seem to fall away when meeting someone for the first time.

You can also put them at ease by asking questions confirming information you have gathered about them and their business from their website, social media, and other online sources. Their website may share the history of the company or the variety of products and services they offer, including some that are outside of the reason you are in their office. Social media sites, like LinkedIn, also provide a history of their business experiences and even other organizations that are important to them.

Take Rapport to a New Level – Build a Bridge of Influence!

As I've developed the skill of connection over the years, I have discovered the process of building rapport with lasting impact is like building a bridge. Engaging the other person in dialogue and creating an opportunity for valued communication requires specific intention.

I think of rapport as *building a bridge of influence.* This means creating an opportunity for value to flow in both directions. Building a bridge between parties allows the two-way flow of influence and makes sure that you are addressing and understanding what your client or customer values most. This helps them determine if your product or service lines up to provide a solution that answers their needs based upon what they value.

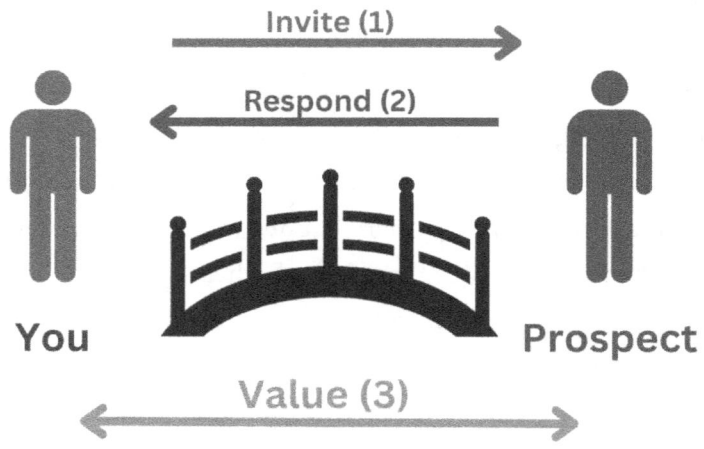

Build a Bridge of Influence

As you can see in the diagram above, there is an important pattern that needs to be followed. Your first step is NOT to tell them what you have to sell or bring to them as a solution. You are not yet able to know what they need or what they value. One of the biggest mistakes I see salespeople make is to assume they know what the prospect's challenges are and what they value most. However, the truth is, you will not fully know until you ask! The following steps will help you build an amazing bridge that allows influence to flow in both directions.

Step 1: Invite (You) – Ask questions inviting them into a dialogue.

- Don't assume anything about your prospects.

- Ask questions to understand and to verify what is going

on in their business and even their life.

- Be Curious! Ask questions and show sincere interest in their responses.
    - Ask about their story.
    - Ask about what they value.
    - Ask about their biggest needs.
    - Ask about their plans for the coming year.

Step 2: Respond (Prospect) – LISTEN! Get in the habit of listening to understand!

- Don't jump ahead and reply or try to solve anything at this time.
- Remain curious and sincerely interested.
- Ask probing questions to gain greater clarity.
    - Ask why that's important to them.
    - Ask if there's a timeline attached to the need.
- Keep your focus on them.

Step 3: Value (Both) – When their responses turn to questions for you, they are indicating their openness to learn more about the value you offer and how it may benefit them.

- This is where the deepest, clearest, and most important conversation happens.

- Don't rush the process! Be patient enough to get here.

- Take special note of what's being said when value is flowing in both directions.

- This is where your customers will get as real as they can with what they want and what they need.

Before you can viably go to the next step in the Five Cs of Every Sales Experience, you need to get this step right. It is the key that unlocks everything else!

Connect - Examples:

The questions you ask can be based around any of the following categories: business experience, family, personal interests, association/affiliations, services, or charities that they are involved in, etc. Observe what you see around their offices and what's posted on the walls, or in frames on a desk or table. See if you can identify with one item and ask them about it. For example:

1 – If you don't mind my asking; tell me, how did you get started in this business?

Or

How did you come to be President of this agency?

(Be careful not to be too cavalier with these questions. Only ask it if you are willing to listen to understand. Also be sure to let your face reflect that you are truly interested!)

This question can help you gain insight into some of the primary motivations and core values of the individual, and it allows you to get to know the foundation and vision they have for themselves and their company. Use your knowledge to make a connection when appropriate and tie your value proposition to their core values. In this way you can demonstrate how you will partner with them to help them accomplish their goals for their business and their team.

2 – I see that you are a member of _____ (industry association/charitable group, etc.).

How long have you been involved with _____?

How has that helped you in growing your business?

How has that benefited you professionally or personally?

This series of questions typically comes from seeing a plaque or certificate on their wall or could even be the result of seeing them at an association event. Their motivation for participating in associations is both business and personal. Many connections come from these groups and most true leaders recognize they can't go it alone in the marketplace. They will need comrades and affiliations which can be sources for referrals that will flow in both directions; out to others and back to them. Being connected to their industry as a business owner is a critical part of the fabric of their success.

3 – Is this your family?

Is this a picture of you coaching soccer?

Are any of your children on the team?

I see that you have played some amazing golf courses.

I see you are a big (sports team) fan!

I remember once asking an agency principal about coaching his son's soccer team. We talked about how much he has enjoyed coaching his youngest son and he was very eager to share the joy this experience has brought to his relationship with his son. He told me about an upcoming tournament they were playing, and I wished him well in that experience.

Forty-five days later I was back in his office and one of the first things I asked him was how the soccer tournament went last month. He paused, looked at me with a curious grin as if to wonder how I knew about it, and then remembered that we had discussed it briefly the last time we saw each other. Because I was sincerely interested in learning more about his coaching and connecting with his son, he went on to share in detail about what an amazing experience it was. He seemed pleased that I listened to him and that I had remembered a specific personal interest of his from our meeting over six weeks earlier. My interest was sincere, and he could tell. Over the next year we enjoyed talking about the responsibility and privilege of raising sons (It certainly helped that he knew I was also the father of four boys). Over the years, we have referred books and experiences back and forth with each other, all of which took our relationship well past business. This individual has become a great friend to me and was willing to share some of his personal contacts and connections with me that helped me grow in business and in life.

PERSPECTIVE Time Out

– Connection questions must be sincere. Remember that they can tell if you really don't care! Don't be that person who asks just to make sure you can check off "building rapport" from your personal agenda for the meeting. One of the greatest ways you can show honor to someone is found in the sincerity of your interest in the other person.

Start by Making the Entire Discussion About Them

When I was asked to speak to a local networking group about the topic of my first book, PEAK PERPSECTIVE, which provides the road map for developing your personal Board of Directors – your own team of mentors – I accepted and asked if we could meet before I spoke at the event. I met Troy Noor, CEO of Boulevard Wealth Management for breakfast. He had heard me speak about this topic a couple of years earlier. I wanted to learn what's been going on in his life and find out why he wanted me to share this particular topic and what he hoped to gain as a result. He told me that after he heard me talk about the importance of having a personal Board of Directors, he wanted to pursue this for his own life and began building his personal board. He said, "Having a personal Board of Directors changed my personal and professional life!"

Troy went on to share that he didn't really know what he had been missing until he asked three men to be on his personal board. They gave him clarity about challenges he was facing, and he appreciated how their wisdom and insight helped him make some important decisions for his business and his personal life. As he shared his personal experience in having a team of mentors, he asked that I share this strategy with this group of local business leaders who need the reminder of the importance of not trying to do everything on their own.

As we continued talking, I asked him about how he strategically connected with his customers and prospects. He said, "Before I say anything about what I do, I make the entire discussion about them." He went on to share that he uses a form as a guide to establish a profile by asking them questions about where they're currently at, where they want to go, and what they ultimately want to accomplish over time. He even presses in on the importance of dreaming about what the future could be. This focus on them takes all the pressure off trying to sell them anything at all. He's simply trying to find out what's most important to them.

Troy's system provides a perfect example of the importance of the first step in building a bridge of influence: focus on discovering what the other person values most. Remember, for each response you get to the questions you initially ask, you are given specific information that helps you ask better questions. As you gain insight into what your customer or prospect values most you are engaging the first step in building a bridge of influence and allowing what they value to flow over to you.

It has been my experience that one of the most important, if not the most important, ingredient in selling is the art of connection. This is the foundation where trust and credibility are built. When you keep your focus on the customer, you will effectively deliver the value they crave.

As outlined in the Essential Selling Perspective framework, what your customer is really looking for is value, service, and trust. Trust comes from being fully engaged in the process of the first two Cs: *Care* and *Connect*. As we proceed through the Five Cs, you'll find they are all essential elements of the process. Don't take for granted the importance of getting started right. Care about your customer and their business and then connect authentically. In the next two chapters, we will shift into the details of the meeting and how to engage your clients and customers to deliver value by meeting their needs.

Sales Perspective Habits

Start
- Get out of your own way and make the entire conversation about them.
- Excell at active listening! Ask questions and listen with the intent to understand.

Analyze
- Throughout the process of connecting think deeply about their biggest needs and keep gathering the necessary information.

Learn
- Let their stories guide you to uncover the specifics of what they're trying to solve.

Engage
- Build a bridge of influence. Be sincere about your interest in them, their business, and their concerns.

Serve
- Let your genuine care for them come through and you will differentiate yourself from the competition.

CLARIFY

VALUE PROPOSITION — SIMPLIFY YOUR MESSAGE

"Clarity Attracts, Confusion Repels." [22]
— Kary Oberbrunner

Lightning Round

"How did you get this number?"

This question caught Terry off guard. All he did that day was call the listed number for a cabinet manufacturer in Princeton, Minnesota. Terry Didion worked for Alexsis, a subsidiary of Alexander & Alexander and represented a self-insured workers' compensation program to agencies and business owners. He was calling to connect with the decision-maker at this organization who might be interested in discussing the benefits of the self-insured program he represented. He was just as surprised as the president of the company that he didn't reach the receptionist. After they both overcame the initial shock of being voice-to-voice, the owner said, "What is it that you are calling about?"

Sensing he was interrupting, Terry got straight to the point. "I am calling to see if you'd be interested in learning about a unique Workers' Compensation program that can benefit your company." The owner jumped in and said, "I already have insurance coverage for my company. I don't have time to listen to a presentation right now." Terry asked if he could set up an appointment to discuss the program. Seizing the opportunity to keep this short, the owner told Terry he would give him one minute to see if he could pique his interest. If Terry succeeded, he would agree to set up a meeting to learn more. Terry agreed. The owner said, "You've got one minute. Go!"

Immediately recognizing there was no time to share a long list of features and benefits, Terry began by asking two questions. He could sense that the owner was looking at his watch and paying extremely close attention to the time. His first question elicited a positive response and Terry asked another question. After responding, the owner said, "Stop!" Terry didn't say another word. He waited for the owner to speak. After a short pause, the owner asked, "Tell me why I shouldn't do this. What's the downside?" Terry simply replied, "You could pay more."

After another short pause, the owner said, "Alright, you've piqued my interest. I will have my assistant reach out to you this afternoon and set an appointment for you to come and see me next week and share the details of this program." Terry shared his contact information and thanked the owner for his time.

Click. Just as quickly as it began, it was over.

What Would You Do with Your Minute?

What if you were in the situation above and you were given one minute to make your case about your product or service to a prospective customer?

Many of you in sales have heard the importance of having some sort of *elevator pitch* in your back pocket to provide a brief overview about what you do when asked. The intent is to force you to get to the heart of the matter and be brief enough to share on a short elevator ride before the door opens and your prospect walks away.

According to the Harvard Office of Career Services, *an elevator pitch is an enticing and interesting three or four-sentence summary of you.* [23]

It never ceases to amaze me how many sales professionals fall prey at some point in their career to sharing their value proposition in the form of a benefits spill. In other words, when they are invited to share their products and services with a prospective customer, they speak from their own perspective hoping something will resonate with their prospects.

Ouch!

I know this pain because I've lived it! Early in my career, I was so enthusiastic about my products and services and how they would bring value, I would dump them onto any prospect that would listen. I felt that if they knew what I knew, they would surely buy from me.

One of the most important perspectives I've learned over my career in sales is that the customer wants you to get to the point. Most business owners are driven to grow and run their business. Don't put them in a position to try and keep up with you. Remember, keep your focus on their perspective and the things you say and do will become more recognizable to them, ultimately helping them assess if you can provide a solution to their needs.

Clarity

Your job is to keep this from being complicated. Make sure to choose your words carefully and line them up with what your prospect has already shared with you! Here are the three primary definitions for clarity to help guide you. Clarity is *the quality of being clear: such as* a) *The quality of being easily understood,* b) *The state of having a full, detailed, and orderly mental grasp of something,* c) *free of confusion.* [24]

Don't make this harder than it needs to be. You have come too far to miss this opportunity. Once you build the bridge of influence and experience the flow of value back and forth with your prospect, it's going to come to your turn to share your solution options with your prospect. As you prepare, set your strategy by doing the following:

1) Plan to take what they share with you and build on it, and

2) Master how you state your value proposition and be ready to share it.

Remember, before you articulate what products or services you have to offer, you must first understand who your client or customer is and what their needs are. Without knowing these details, your message is irrelevant! To the best of your ability, make sure that you uncover what is most important to them! This is about them first and foremost.

CHALLENGE: If you go into a prospect meeting beating your chest about all that you have to offer them and you don't know whether you're even speaking to the decision-maker or what their needs are, you will miss the mark every time. This is not about you, your product or service, or about what you have to say.

SOLUTION: Clarity calls you to keep it simple. Some would even suggest using this reminder as you approach an opportunity to communicate by using the K.I.S.S method. This stands for: Keep It Simple Sweetheart! Over my career, I have kept the idea of clarity and simplicity in focus by reminding myself that what I have to say is not as important as what they need to hear.

Of course, you will never know what they need to hear until you clarify who they are and what they need. Set your ego and your own bravado aside and focus on your prospect. Once you get to know them, understand that you are still not finished learning about their wants and needs. You need to continue clarifying their perspective in each subsequent meeting. Don't ever get caught assuming you know what's most important to them or that nothing has changed since you last connected with them.

Remember to be clear and concise in your message! Let's examine the fundamentals of communicating value to your prospects and customers.

Value Proposition

This is about *your* message. Once you have a grasp on what is most important to your prospect or customer, you can find the areas of opportunity where your products and services intersect with their needs. If you want to make your message clear, take a few minutes, and ask yourself the following questions, reflecting on the importance of clarity in your responses and making note of the most concise way to deliver your message:

Q: What is my value proposition?

A: The detailed description of the value my product or service delivers to meet the needs of my prospects and customers.

Q: What do I do with it?

A: Communicate the value of the product/service I provide and how it can make a positive difference for my client/customer.

Q: Why is it so important to be clear and concise in my messaging?

A: My prospects are looking for specific solutions and not general dialogue.

Q: Why should being 'clear and concise' stand out as a primary component of my value proposition?

A: Clarity attracts – Confusion repels. I need to know my messaging in the most concise way possible. Remember to be straight forward first. I can always expound on more details if needed or requested.

Less is More

Believe it or not, I could go on talking and telling three to five relevant anecdotes or analogies for almost any situation—it's the blessing and curse of my personality and my experience. The real key to clarity is not in how much you say but what you choose to say—or not say—that makes all the difference. Being clear and concise is a skill that comes from practice. Bringing clarity to a situation starts with knowing the needs of your client, how your products or services may help them, and sharing *only* the necessary information to help them solve their issues or needs.

Clarity comes from integrating the questions you've been asking throughout the conversation and the specific solutions your products or services may offer to your customers. To deliver a valued message to your clients, don't fall prey to making assumptions. As you learn what their needs are and what they are trying to accomplish, keeping your focus on their needs is a key fundamental to gaining clarity in what they want and what you say.

Making assumptions about what your client wants leads mostly to missed opportunities. When you fill in the answer to a question that should be reserved for your client, you fail to understand what their needs really are. How can you bring clarity to someone when what you are saying doesn't line up with their needs?

If you want clarity, ask questions. If you want to understand your client's needs, ask them for more information. You have a great opportunity to take this process to the next level.

In his book *Day Job to Dream Job*, Kary Oberbrunner shared a simple message that has impacted me greatly and helped me understand the importance of clarity. He said,

"Clarity Attracts – Confusion Repels." [25]

Over the years, I have gained a better understanding of this principle. When I heard it stated in such a simple and clear fashion it rocked me! When I adopted it in my strategy for every connection, my results were transformed! Know that your prospect wants to get to the heart of the matter. When aiming for the heart of your message remember to be clear and concise. This will give you the best opportunity to have the greatest transfer of value to your clients. The simpler you keep it, the greater your chances are of achieving clarity! When your tendency starts to lean into more stories, follow these two steps and gain clarity in your understanding of their needs and deliver with clarity the solutions that fit them.

Step 1: Clarify what their needs are—be specific!

Step 2: Be clear and concise about how your product or service meets their needs.

As I shared with your earlier in the book about the lessons learned following my "Diffusing the Bear" story, one of the most effective ways that I have found to keep me focused on choosing the right words to communicate with clarity is embracing the guiding perspective that *what I have to say is not as important as what they need to hear.* This really works! Take your time in choosing the right words and you will strike gold with clarity. It may seem counterintuitive to think that less words can add more value, but it works. Your customer will find themselves wanting to work with you when you are clear and concise. This is a powerful way to keep adding value to them.

Add Value

As I mentioned in Chapter Three, Rick Larson was my boss and an invaluable mentor to me. He taught me a lot about effective communication and quality presentations. I had the privilege of working alongside Rick as he hosted a training program he developed called *Stand Up and Speak*. This course was designed to identify prospective instructors for the licensing and continuing education classes that Prosource offered for Real Estate, Insurance, Appraisal, and Contractors.

Rick delivered a perspective that has stuck with me all these years and it is absolutely true. Once I understood the difference between these two styles, I made a shift in my presentation style that allowed me to make greater connections and have a deeper impact. He taught that there are typically two types of approaches that presenters use:

The Hammer & Nail versus The Individual Chair

1. The Hammer & Nail

   This presenter operates on the philosophy: "I'm a hammer and all the world is a nail! If I pound into you everything I know, you will be better off as a result." This type of presentation is all about the presenter and what they know.

2. The Individual Chair

   This presenter believes that the most important perspective belongs to the person sitting in the individual chairs in the room. This presenter's philosophy sounds like: "If I could know and understand what's most important to each person in this room, I would be in a position to add the most value to them today." This type of presentation is focused on the people in the room. It starts with taking account of what they need and how you can send them away with the kind of value that will have a positive impact on their business.

You should always position your sales presentation to have an impact on each attendee, whether it be in front of a larger group, meeting with a prospect and their team, or an individual prospect. Your goal should be to make sure they leave the room better off than before they showed up. The best way to deliver a valued outcome comes from spending time learning the greatest challenges the attendees face in their industry and how best to solve them. You can't know everything, but you can add value by getting to know the most common challenges. This information can often be found through local and regional associations for their industry. Align what you learn with the structure of your presentation and your questions will become more specific and relevant, helping you connect with your prospects and customers. When you have a chance to get in front of your clients or prospects, your perspective matters. Here's the key:

You will provide the greatest value when you position your presentation to the perspective of what's most important to your customer!

Being Concise

I used to work for a company where we had a team of people from different departments meet and present the various details of the program we represented to prospective clients. With five main categories, each with its unique value components to the overall value proposition, each of us would take turns presenting these components to prospects. I built this as a specific strategy that worked very well, especially when we listened to the prospects' questions and issues and then tailored our presentation to address the specific needs of the company/owner.

One of the presenters needed coaching to keep him on track and honor the prospects' time. This individual was knowledgeable and well-spoken, yet consistently went over his allotted time in our presentations. During a coaching session as we prepared for another presentation, I approached him about the importance of conveying the critical details of his department in a concise manner. He said he would try his best to keep to the time and then said something I will never forget. He said, "You have to understand, I come by it honestly. There are so many facets of this department that it's hard to keep it as narrow as you are asking. Besides, I have always lived by the credo, 'why use 50 words when 150 will do!'"

Is it true that less is more? I must admit that I want to answer "Yes" right away to that question, yet the reality is, it depends. If you want to be clear in your message, be brutally honest with yourself about your presentation. What is critical? What can be left out? In other words, know the difference between good-to-know and need-to-know. A strong analogy is valuable when properly applied to your point. Three analogies are overkill! Remember that you are not trying to drum it into their head. You are simply trying to be clear in making your point. What you say also confirms to them that you've been listening to them. Communicating back to them with clarity helps them see that you are there to potentially provide a solution to *their* needs. Being clear and concise is your friend and enhances your ability to confirm their buy-in to your ideas.

Let's break conciseness down to the basics. Ask yourself the following questions when determining the essential elements of your message.

- How many main points do I have?
- How many do I need?
- What is the most important element of my value?
- What do I need to know from my client before I can prescribe a solution?
- Does my *main thing* line up with my client's *main thing*?
- What would my presentation look like if I had to deliver it in half the time I usually use?
- What has to stay?
- What must go?
- How can I make my point with fewer words?
- Is there an example I can use that incorporates all the elements I need to cover?
- If your client said, "The shorter this is the better your chances are with me today," what would you change?
- If you could ask only one question before presenting your plan, what would you ask?

Time

Make "time" your friend and ally. What do I mean by that? You need to elevate the importance of time and not depend on your client to do it for you. You are always better off leaving before they expect rather than staying longer than they want! One of my favorite examples of what it means to honor someone else's time comes from Frank Bettger in his book *How I Raised Myself from Failure to Success in Selling*. He shares an experience in which he learned how to effectively set an appointment with a busy business owner and honor his time in the process. Bettger reached out by phone to a potential customer, Mr. Aley, who was referred to him by another friend. Upon introducing himself on the phone he mentioned that they had a mutual friend who suggested they get to know each other. He acknowledged that Mr. Aley was a busy man and asked for five minutes of his time one day this week.

After confirming he was not trying to sell him anything, Bettger asked if he could stop by and see him tomorrow morning at nine o'clock. Here is Bettger describing the rest of the story:

> *Aley: I have an appointment for nine-thirty.*
> *Me: Well, if I take longer than five minutes, it will be your fault not mine.*
> *Aley: All right. You'd better make it nine-fifteen.*
> *Me: Thank you, Mr. Aley. I'll be there.*

The next morning as I shook hands with him in his office, I took out my watch and said: "You've got another appointment at nine-thirty, so I'm going to limit myself to exactly five minutes."

I went through my questions as briefly as I could. When my five minutes were gone I said: "Well, my five minutes are up. Is there anything else you would like to tell me, Mr. Aley?" And for the next ten minutes Mr. Aley told me all I really wanted to know about him.
26

What I learned about the importance of time from this example—along with lots of trial and error—is to use the time to my advantage. When I set a time parameter for a meeting, it forces me to limit what I have to say. It's perfectly fine to have an agenda to guide your discussion, however, you can't have too many items on your list.

Believe it or not, filling up the allotted time is not your goal. Honoring their time is paramount. It's okay to finish up early. It sends an important message when you wrap up a particular meeting before the completion of the time you requested. You are choosing to honor their time, not just fill it.

Depending on the length of time you preset for your meeting, you should keep your agenda to two to three items. This allows for specific purpose in the meeting and time to handle additional questions or specific issues from your customer that need your attention.

The Gatekeeper

Have you ever shared your product or service with someone who has to go to someone else to get an answer or decision regarding your offer? If you're used to dealing directly with the decision-maker, this can seem like a frustrating position. When communicating with a gatekeeper, you can't ask any clarifying questions to get the owner's perspective. It is common for the representative to have a list of questions you are expected to answer, where your answers will be compiled along with the other suitors and reported to the owner. Rather than let this become a barrier to your message, I suggest you let clarity be your strongest asset in this scenario.

Use this simple three-step process: *Challenge—Solution—Outcome.* This formula will allow you to set the table with a common challenge question, the best solution for the problem and the ultimate result of implementing the solution. Remember back in Chapter 3 when we talked about the "Telephone Game?" This is how you overcome the miscommunication that can come from speaking to a representative and not the decision-maker.

I suggest coming up with two to three common problems facing the business or industry your prospect is in and present them this way:

1. If your most important concern is _____ *(primary challenge)*, then you should choose _____ *(primary solution)*, as this will have the strongest positive impact on _____ *(outcome)* in the coming year!

2. If your most important concern is _____ *(secondary challenge)*, then you should choose _____ *(secondary solution)*, as this will have the strongest positive impact on _____ *(outcome)* in the coming year!

3. If your most important concern is _____ *(other challenge)*, then you should choose _____ *(other solution)*, as this will have the strongest positive impact on _____ *(outcome)* in the coming year!

This pattern gives you the ability to uncover the primary challenge they face and the
ultimate solution they desire. Remember that the first response isn't always the real issue of greatest concern to your prospect. Asking the three questions above helps you discover which challenge is the most important one to overcome.

Do Your Homework

The importance of the work you do in advance of meeting with your prospect, like the CARE you have for them and their business as we discussed in Chapter 6, provides you the ability to know and understand the biggest issues they face.

This allows you the opportunity to paint the pictures of the *Challenge—Solution—Outcome* in situations they will be able to understand.

Sales Perspective Habits

Start
- Start with the idea that less is more and begin to take clarity seriously.
- Focus on being brief and clear.

Analyze
- Spend time on the examples and analogies you typically use and ask yourself if you could only use one, which one would it be.

Learn
- Let the responses they provide guide you in shaping the one example that will resonate with the problem they are trying to solve.

Engage
- When it's your turn to speak, focus on being clear and concise.

Serve
- Ask for their understanding along the way. This helps to keep your focus on them.

Confirm

ACCURACY —
REVIEW AND ACKNOWLEDGE UNITY

"A salesperson cannot know too much, but he or she can talk too much." [27]

— Frank Bettger

Missed Cues

It was hard to watch.

I WAS INVITED BY one of my agents to present my workers' compensation program to a prospective customer. The agent was scheduled to present the products and services his agency would provide to this prospect, should they decide to work with him. This was a new relationship opportunity for the agent, and I was asked to present the details of my program first as a portion of the overall coverage the company needed. I asked the owner a few specific questions and then addressed them with how this program was designed to help solve the issues this company was facing.

After my portion of the presentation was completed, the agent went on to the other lines of coverage this company would need to protect their operation. The agent shared examples and details about his other business accounts and the service he would commit to provide if the owner was willing to give him an opportunity to quote his business. Within about twenty minutes, this business owner was asking questions and giving indications that he wanted to have this agent quote his business. There was only one problem. The agent wouldn't stop talking! He addressed one line of coverage and then told a story about it. Another line of coverage, another story.

Over the course of the next 10 minutes, I watched the business owner change in temperament and attention. Finally, he interrupted the agent and told him he needed to think about it. The agent was stunned and asked why he needed to think about it. The owner told him he wanted to discuss it with some of his colleagues and other owners and get back to him with a decision about moving ahead. We thanked the owner for his time and attention and left the meeting.

Out in the parking lot, the agent was surprised and confused as to what had happened. He asked me for my observations, and I shared that it appeared to me that he didn't seem to recognize when the owner was giving him buying signals. I told him he was too far away for me to kick him under the table, but the unending stories seemed to disengage the owner, and he slowly lost interest.

As I thought about this situation later, it occurred to me the owner was likely questioning whether he wanted to do business with an agent that was more enamored with the sound of his own voice than the specific needs of the customer.

Lesson Learned

Yes, it was tough to watch and hard feedback to share with the agent. I was not surprised when the business owner declined to move forward with this agent. It was almost surreal to watch as the agent talked himself into and out of the opportunity in less than 45 minutes.

I learned a valuable lesson from this experience and have since made it a point to keep the focus on the prospect throughout a meeting. Remember, as the meeting time is coming to close, stop yourself from going on and on. The confirmation step calls you to create unity around what was discussed and focus on the areas where your products or services address the needs of your customer.

As we learned in the previous chapter, confusion repels people away from the solutions you offer. The confirmation step is the time to stick to an accurate review of the items you discussed and the potential they have to deliver a solution to your customer's primary needs.

Make sure you confirm a complete buy-in to the game plan that was discussed. No shortcuts! If you have made a connection, identified the issues, and clearly and concisely communicated how your product or service can help, then complete the picture by asking affirming questions to receive their unified understanding of summary of the conversation.

Don't skimp on this step! You must close the loop and confirm their buy-in to your message and your solution. You may want to provide support materials or offer them your partnership in delivering the message to any other team members before they make a decision.

Resist the temptation to jump too quickly to close the deal. Instead, strive to close any gaps in understanding to confirm you are together in your thinking.

When reviewing the information you've learned throughout the sales experience up to this point, it's helpful to put the word – confirm – in the proper context. Confirm means 1) *to give approval to, ratify;* 2) *to make firm or firmer, strengthen;* 3) *to give new assurance of the validity of, remove doubt about by authoritative act or indisputable fact.* [28]

Take these elements and make sure you are ratifying, strengthening, and validating all that has been discussed and discovered throughout the conversation. Simply put, confirm they are on the same page as you. This is accomplished by asking them to affirm statements you make about what you heard them say in discussing the issues they are facing and the solutions for which they are searching.

Don't assume anything. Don't let your guard down, especially when you're in a hurry. Don't let assumptions get you into trouble. Often by the time you get to this stage, you'll find that your customer has confirmed in their own mind they want to work with you. Your task at this point is to have them say it out loud. The best method is to simply review all the points in the conversation and make sure that you are both clear about the direction you're heading.

Review Key Solutions

Throughout my career in sales, I have heard the importance of staying on track and avoiding over-talking by adhering to the following admonition by Stephen Covey:

__Keep the Main Thing, the Main Thing!__[29]

As easy as it is to get sidetracked on the details, when providing a summary review to your customer, stick to the main topics. As we discussed in the last chapter, I have learned to use the following framework to help keep me on track. I start by structuring the review narrative to reflect the following sequence:

Challenge — Solution — Outcome.

This paints the picture of a process of identifying exactly what the client's biggest challenge is, applying the proper solution to it, and the transformation realized by the outcome. Once I understood the impact of this pattern, I began consistently speaking in terms of the customer's outcome.

For example, I might say something like:

"What this will mean to ... (you, your bottom line, your cash flow, your efficiency, etc.)."

"As a result of ..."

"Once you implement ..."

"You can expect ..."

Remember to frame your narrative to reflect the *Challenge — Solution — Outcome* pattern always keeping your focus on the outcome. What you are doing is showing them what the future may hold for them and their organization when they take the next step.

Paint the Picture

This is where stories become an effective tool in communication. Use the power of stories to tell them about their potential future. In her best-selling book *Stories THAT Stick*, Kindra Hall provides a proven framework to help us all take appropriate advantage of the power of stories. When it comes to The Value Story, Hall shares the importance of what lies beyond the features and benefits or other metrics of our products or services. "On the other side of those metrics, is a person. A person with a problem. A person who needs you to solve that problem. A person who needs a story to captivate them, assure them your solution is the right one, and turn them into a believer." [30]

This clearly indicates the limiting nature of sharing only the features and benefits of your products or services. The limited view of only discussing what your product is or does is technical and often misses the mark when you're trying to connect with your customer.

I like to think of it this way:

When you make them the main character in a story about their future state that includes the solution to their specific issues, you've got their attention.

PERSPECTIVE Time Out

– Be careful! This step is often confused with engaging closing strategies. Don't do it. Don't change the environment you have built through these first four steps in the process. Confirmation is simply affirming them through common agreement. Remember that your goal is to keep them believing that you are there to serve them, not sell them. Confirm that they understand where they are in the process and make sure to take this time address and uncover any lingering questions.

Your Purpose Explained

Reinforce that you are there to help them make the best decision for their business. One of the strategies I have used to great effect is to position myself as an assistant buyer.

In his book, *How I Raised Myself From Failure to Success In Selling*, Frank Bettger recounts the success behind a large sale he made, pointing to a posture that has helped me focus on my role in the sales process. He states that one of the four rules that helped him gain the stranger's confidence was to *Be an Assistant Buyer*.

Here are the details of his thinking, in his own words:

> *"In preparation for the interview, I imagined myself a salaried employee of Mr. Booth's company. I assumed the role of "assistant buyer in charge of insurance." In this matter my knowledge was superior to Mr. Booth's. Feeling this way, I didn't hesitate to put all the enthusiasm and excitement I could command into what I said. That idea helped me to be absolutely fearless. The assistant buyer attitude was such a definite help to me in that sale that I have kept right on through the years playing that role ... People don't like to be sold. They like to buy."* [31]

The idea of taking the posture of an assistant buyer was so impactful to my way of thinking, that it became a vital part of what I call taking a *Posture of Partnership*. The posture you take is often built into the words you say and the way you ask questions. It may not always be a physical posture, standing or sitting next to your prospect, and is more likely to be a verbal and mental posture. This involves the type of questions you ask and the way you invite them into unity or agreement about their understanding of the options before them. Remember this posture of partnership is you pointing them to their choices for a potential solution so *they* can make the best decision for their business. It also has the effect of removing the feeling that they are being sold.

> **Posture of Partnership:** *Become an Assistant Buyer*
> - Come alongside your prospect and review the information...
>
> - So they can make the best decision for their business...
>
> - It removes the felling they are being sold.

When people get the sense that your posture is to make sure they are heard and not manipulated, they tend to listen to your solutions with a welcome attitude. When you stick to helping *them* make the best decision for *their* business, they'll see you as a valued partner to their business. Remember this truth. People don't like to be sold. They like to buy.

Confirming is summarizing the discussion and questions into the salient points that matter most to your prospect. When you arrive at common agreement, they are more likely to take the next step with you when you keep the focus on them. I have found many times that as I wrap up the confirmation process, my prospect is ready to make a commitment. Sometimes that commitment is to go to the next step in gathering information or the next step in completing the deal. Don't rush or push them to make a decision. Simply keep the confirmation process clear and they will stay with you to the next step.

Sales Perspective Habits

Start
- Strive to keep your summaries on the topic at hand.

Analyze
- Set aside any old scripts you would have used to move toward closing and simply review what's already been discussed.
- Ask for confirmation about their understanding throughout the summary.

Learn
- Pay attention to their body language and general demeanor.
- Learn to point the summary topics toward their solution.

Engage
- Embrace the *Posture of Partnership* as an assistant buyer.
- Be natural in your delivery. You are simply building on the relationship you've already established.
- If they indicate they need clarity on a particular item, take the time on the spot to provide it to them.

Serve
- Remember who you're there for.
- They will also know by your focus, so keep it on them.

COMMIT

SPECIFIC NEXT STEPS — AGREED UPON OUTCOME

"It was character that got us out of bed, commitment that moved us into action, and discipline that enabled us to follow through." [32]

— Zig Ziglar

My Mistake

"I'll get back to you after I discuss this with my partner." How did I miss that important piece of information? In my early days of sales, I didn't even think to ask if there was anyone else in the company that would have input on the decision about moving forward. I set the appointment with the person who I thought was the decision-maker.

My mistake. Or was it?

In a world where some people don't like to be sold or talked into making a commitment or sales decision, they use one of many defensive tactics to postpone a decision until they've had a chance to review all their options. This strategy does have some merit; however, it is most often born out of a sense of buyer's remorse from their past.

If you trust your product and your process, then the only "ask" you have of them is "What's next?" Remember, you are not just focusing on striving to close the deal and complete a sale at this point. You are still building a partnership and must keep your mind on what's most important to them, even when it involves waiting. One way I've found to help relieve the stress and pressure of a decision is to make the next step simple.

Commit

The Five Cs of Every Sales Experience doesn't end with a traditional closing strategy, but rather concludes with making a commitment. To commit means, 1) *to carry into action deliberately,* 2) *to obligate or bind,* 3) *to pledge or assign to some particular course or use.* [33]

Your goal is to build a partnership with your prospect or customer. Commit to serve them! This means train them, walk alongside them, help them accomplish what they want as your paramount purpose. When pledging a particular course of action for them, make sure to make your commitment first and invite them to join you in the next step. When you invite them to continue the journey, it confirms for them that what you want is the best for them. When you turn this step into serving them, they'll want to do business with you because you're not like most other sales professionals trying to talk them into something.

In the next chapter we will discuss the strategy and skills needed to handle objections and bring your value into focus for your customers. When you choose to honor them with your commitment to service, they will thank you for your honesty and candor.

Your Next Best Step

Continuing to create buy-in along the way doesn't stop at the Confirm step. When it comes to making a commitment, I've found that striving for a mutual commitment is a sign of partnership building. Seeking some form of commitment from your prospect or customer is always necessary, even when it seems daunting.

This strategy goes beyond simply asking them what they want. It's asking them what they think the next step is for them. I have found that a question positioned to seek their input acts as an invitation. I might simply ask something like, "As you are evaluating your options, what would you consider to be *your next best step*?"

As you listen to their response, take what they give you and then share a mutual commitment option. It could sound like this, "Based on what we've discussed today and the questions you raised, I will commit to getting the complete answers for you on those topics. I'd also ask that you verify the answers to my questions about timing and anyone else who should be involved in the process. Are there any other items you'd like to include in this next step?" Don't ask for a pending decision to be made at any time. You're only inviting them to commit to the next step. Rather than impose any heavy pressure, I'm inviting them to press on for more clarity. That's the only commitment I'm asking of them.

Outcome Equals Value

It's easy to get caught up in the transaction at this point in the sales experience. However, I encourage you to remember that any outcome you're striving for should be based on the value you bring to your customer. Any decision made by your customer at this point is primarily based on the value you displayed in helping them solve their problem. You should want their decision to buy based on their choice and not your strategy to close. I know this sounds unconventional. Over time, you'll find that when you keep your focus on the best outcome for them, it's less of a strategy and more of a conversation.

In his book *The Only Sales Guide You'll Ever Need*, Anthony Iannarino offers the insight that what you're really selling is not your product or service, it's the outcome. Iannarino says, "Today, success in sales requires much more of you, the salesperson, for you are a large part of the value proposition. Your client is buying not just the outcome, but *your* ability to deliver it. This means that you have to own the outcome, not just the sale." Of course this means all of the details fall under your authority. He goes on to encourage you to work diligently with your team and your client's team to deliver the promised outcome. Iannarino says it this way, "When you deliver what you're truly selling—a successful outcome—you build a strong reputation as someone who fulfills his or her promises." [34]

You'll end up delivering the best results for your customers when you keep them thinking about what their future looks like with the problem solved. This is where they end up embracing the next step. Whether it's for more information, a buying commitment, or final negotiation, always keep their eyes on the outcome of the value they'll receive. This helps avoid any major issues of buyer's remorse.

The Invitation

Think about it this way. Have you ever heard about a party or gathering that happened and you didn't get invited? How did that make you feel?

- Did you feel seen?

- Did you feel wanted?

- Did you feel valued?

- Did you feel connected?

Like most people, you probably would say no to most, if not all, of the questions above. Everyone likes to be invited. When you invite them to join you in committing to the next step, it means you see them, you want them included, you value their input, you want to stay connected to make sure they experience the maximum value they are looking for, including the proper solution to their biggest needs.

When you invite them to join you in making a commitment to the next best step, they will buy into the journey they are already on with you. If you leave them off the hook in making a commitment, they may feel like you aren't focused enough on their needs. Assure them that is not the case by taking the first step in making a commitment to the next step, then invite them to join you. This connection strategy, just like in step number two, is the key to a strong bond. Sales is a relationship business. You need to strive to work well and get along with others. Remember that being genuine, sincere, and authentic builds the bond with your customer faster than any product can. Yes, people want solutions. People also crave relationships with people they can trust.

When you are genuine, sincere, and authentic in the first four Cs, this last one naturally comes together. It is the culmination of handling the first four properly and with integrity.

Don't Be Surprised

As you come alongside your prospect in the process, don't be surprised if the majority of the time the prospect or customer agrees to complete the deal in this step. It won't necessarily take a long time for them to make a commitment if you have treated them well throughout the process. Building trust relationships has many advantages for your prospects and customers. Especially when they feel connected to you as their trusted advisor. A trusted advisor is a common label associated with your role in creating a powerful bond with your prospect. When you bring people to the point of trusting you with their concerns and ideas about what is needed to solve their issues, you are on your way to building a relationship where commitment doesn't feel forced or coerced. This is the best place to be in a relationship. Remember to avoid thinking about the transaction and keep the language you choose focused on them and their needs.

It is also common for the sale to close itself along the way and this step is simply putting the final touches on the deal they are looking for.

This is Not The End

As a sales professional, you must understand that the agreed upon outcome is not the end of the process or the sale. If you agree on making the next best step, it's just the next step. You need to keep going. Keep delivering service. Keep asking questions. Keep listening with the intent to understand.

Using the **Five Cs of Every Sales Experience** to provide a road map you can customize to your own business and personality will lead you to deliver a lasting impact on the lives you connect with on your journey. You will make a difference when you are strategic and intentional about adding value to others. When you serve their needs and put them above your own needs, you will always win.

PERSPECTIVE Time Out

– What about asking for an annual volume commitment from your customer? In a representative selling model (B2B4C), it's a common practice to have requirements by your company to set annual goals with your existing client base. It's easy to fall into a strategy of identifying the goal you want them to attain based upon their previous years accomplishments or deficiencies. Rather than press in on a number they need to hit in the coming year, I suggest you try the invitation pattern from above. In other words, invite them to join you in the pursuit of growth for the coming year. I have used this strategy to great effect over the years. When you are told to get them to commit to a number, remember that the number is not the focus. You should address the opportunity to invite them to join you on the same page regarding the strategy or plan for the coming months.

It might sound something like this, "As we look to identify an appropriate growth goal in the year ahead, I don't want you to focus on the number as much as your commitment to the trajectory of where we can go together. My commitment to you is to help you accomplish your goals. My request of you is to work with me and provide access to your team periodically to make sure we are all on the same page and moving toward the same goal."

Be careful not to fall into the trap of asking for a commitment to a sales or volume goal with your client too early. If they give you a commitment without knowing what the game plan is or how you are going to help them accomplish their goals, you are only getting a hollow value in the "commitment" they supposedly made.

That might seem callous and insincere, but it's the truth. I have seen firsthand how the business owner will make a commitment only because he knows that the sales rep has to fill out a report for his boss to see that he got the commitment to a certain dollar amount from the client.

If you start your conversation with your client and tell them this is a planning session, then keep your word. Stick to the plan unless they invite you to go further.

Sales Perspective Habits

Start
- Set the path for their next step.

Analyze
- Let them decide what they want to do next.
- If they are unsure, go back and confirm each element again.

Learn
- If there is more than one decision-maker and one is not present, set up the next appointment to discuss the options with them included.

Engage
- Be flexible. Don't push. Listen as much as you can to them and any signals they provide about what they are still missing or may want to do next.

Serve
- Leave the ultimate decision in their hands.
- Remember, people don't like to be sold, they like to buy.

FINISH WELL

HANDLING OBJECTIONS — FOLLOW UP AND FOLLOW THROUGH

> *"I also realize that winning doesn't always mean getting first place; it means getting the best out of yourself."*[35]
>
> — Meb Keflezighi, 2004 Olympic Marathon silver medalist

Persevere to the End

During the Big Ten Indoor Track Championships, in 2008, Heather Dorniden accomplished what seemed impossible after falling near the end of the second lap of the 600-meter race. As a celebrated runner for the University of Minnesota, Dorniden, found herself moving into the lead with 200 meters to go when she tripped after contacting the foot of another runner. She fell to the ground landing hard, as the other three runners, including one of her teammates, sprinted ahead and into the lead. Rather than give up, or stay down, Dorniden jumped to her feet and took off running. Sprinting around the track as the last lap was in progress, it seemed surreal as she was gaining speed and rapidly closed the gap between her and the other three competitors. Coming around the final turn, she had moved into third place and was sprinting all out as she passed the other two runners, including her teammate to win the race! This amazing feat of skill, courage, and heart was on full display for all to see, including her family and friends as this was a home field meet held at the University of Minnesota.

In an interview after the race, Heather was quoted as saying, "I knew team points were close, so there was never any doubt that I would finish the race. Luckily, it was a home meet, so my whole team, my parents, and fans gave me so much energy. I heard the announcer say, 'Watch out for Heather Dorniden.' I thought, yeah, watch out for Heather." [36] This incredible display of perseverance and overcoming adversity was and continues to be an inspiration to many.

You can check out the video of this amazing feat on YouTube.com titled: *Heather Dorniden Wins the Race.* [37]

This example begs the question, "What would you do if you got sidetracked or even fell down during your race to get where you wanted to go?" Maybe you're not competing in a race, but just trying to accomplish a task or achieve a goal that you set for yourself. Does a setback stop you? Are you thrown from your game? Are you quick to give up? Are you busy looking for the reset button or content to try again some other time? Or are you willing to do whatever it takes to accomplish your goal and finish well?

Do you have to win the race to celebrate your accomplishment? Is it possible to "win" at the race by persevering to the end and finishing the race, even if you come in last? Absolutely! Your energy and effort are part of the contest and determine much about you and your character. Yes, everyone wants to win the race, or in sales, the deal, but don't think for a moment that being in the race and giving it your all is not important.

The Importance of Finishing Well

In sports, business, and in life, finishing well has great importance. As in the story above regarding the incredible recovery by Dorniden, overcoming obstacles and pressing on until the end, can result in amazing accomplishments. Another common practice in team sports is the idea of the *fourth quarter*. As a sign of perseverance and unity to the end of the game, when the fourth quarter begins, teams would put up four fingers to remind everyone that the fourth quarter was their time to shine! This is where teams would push themselves to a new level of energy and focus, just like they had been training to do. It fueled them to dig deeper and press harder into their very best effort. This would often propel them past the teams that hadn't trained for the stamina and durability required in the fourth quarter of the game.

In business, entering the fourth quarter of the sales year invokes a sense of urgency and focus to finish the year well. The impact may be related to profitability, qualifying for annual bonuses, or meeting new production numbers. These motivations move people differently, yet, as is most common in sales, the end of the year also signals the end of the production cycle. When a New Year starts, everyone begins at zero and strives to launch high in the upcoming year.

When it comes to life, we only have one life to live. How we live it, and who and what we live for matters more as we age. I often think about what it means to live life today with an eye toward the future. *What can I do today that will impact the generations to come? Will I be remembered? Will my life have meaning to my loved ones, friends, or even my colleagues?*

These types of questions bring into focus what matters most and elevate the importance of finishing well. How we choose to finish well in life carries over to all areas of importance, such as, family, relationships, faith, career, community, or country.

How You Finish Matters

In sales, the greatest value is found not only in how you start, but also in how you finish. Is it only about winning the sale or is the journey also important?

Consider this: *Can you hold your head high when you've done everything to the best of your ability and still not closed the deal?*

If you are wondering whether the answer to that question is yes or no, you may need to look inside yourself to determine if you've addressed every element that is in your control to the best of your ability.

One of the biggest battles in sales is holding yourself accountable to things you cannot control. When something is outside of your control, don't fall into the trap of trying to solve it. Worrying about what you can't control is a wasted effort. Embrace the fact that you can't control what you can't control! However, what you can control is where you focus your effort. Hold yourself accountable to the things you can control and focus on what works in that area. This is where you learn to understand what you did and if you handled all of it to the best of your ability.

Another important component in measuring how we finish well is the role of integrity. To be specific, integrity is defined as 1) *an adherence to moral and ethical principles; soundness of moral character; honesty;* 2) *the state of being whole, entire, or undiminished.* [38]

Integrity helps us look at everything we've been through and determine if we've remained consistent throughout the process. In the event of multiple challenges, it helps us measure how we performed emotionally, intellectually, and strategically when we realize that we handled all elements that were in our control. In other words, even when we lose the sale, we still win if we've done everything in our power the right way.

The purpose and intent of being guided by integrity is described well by Dr. Henry Cloud in his book, *Integrity,* as he shares some additional definitions and their proper application.

"And, the origins of the word we can see in the French and Latin meanings of *intact, integrate, integral,* and *entirety.* The concept means that the 'whole thing is working well, undivided, integrated, intact, and uncorrupted.' When we are talking about integrity, we are talking about being a whole person, an integrated person, with all our different parts working well and delivering the functions that they were designed to deliver. It is about wholeness and effectiveness as people. It truly is 'running on all cylinders.'" [39]

How Do You Want to Be Known?

Whether you are cleaning the garage, cutting the grass, throwing a ball, or swinging a bat, tennis racket, or golf club, one of the important elements of completing the overall process is to follow through.

When it comes to character, there are typically two types of people in this world. Those who have character, and those that *are* characters! This is a lesson I learned from my parents when I was growing up. The inference here is that the people with character can be depended upon to follow through with their commitments, are considered people of their word, and are dependable and reliable. On the other hand, those who *are* characters are more likely to be gregarious, playful, unpredictable, foolish, care-free, inconsistent, and unreliable.

I admit that it took me a while to understand the difference. Over the years I have confessed to my parents that I chose to be a character-hybrid. I wanted to be a man of character (dependable / reliable / consistent) *and* be a character (playful and engaging / have fun along the way).

I came to understand that being a man of character meant that I must be a man of my word; that I could be trusted to follow through and do what I said I would do. In sales, learning trust and earning trust comes *after* completing the transaction. It's not the sale that makes you a person of your word. It's how you handle all phases of the sale, including how you follow up and follow through, that spreads the word and allows others to identify you in the way that you want to be known.

Back in Chapter 1 we saw how author Jeff Henderson pointed us to understand the most important ingredient in the growth of our business is our customers. This idea laid the groundwork for helping us focus on utilizing the proper perspective for our business success. But wait, there's more!

As we learn to finish well, Henderson uses the customer's perspective to help us contemplate two questions: "What do we want to be known FOR?" and "What *are* we know FOR?" [40] The underlying idea is learning the difference between what we want to be known for in the marketplace, and what our customers say we are known for. If you want to finish well, you'll need to focus on the actual outcome more than your desired outcome when it comes to your reputation. You can only arrive at what you want your reputation to be when you line up your perspective with the perspective your customers have of you.

Be The Difference

How do you make a difference in the eyes of your prospects and customers? How do you stand out in a world vying for their attention? Like most everything in life, it starts with you. You make the difference. It's not what you offer, it's who you are and how you treat them. If you want to make a difference, be the difference!

In a world of obligations and responsibilities, you have the opportunity to be the difference by changing your narrative, your attitude, and your outcome. Rather than listing all the things you have to do, start looking at your list as things you *get* to do. You get to make connections. You get to stand in the gap between your customer and their desired solution. You get to ask questions and listen to them to discover what it is they really want. You get to show them you care about them and their business by how you treat them.

You get to be the difference in their lives by understanding what it is they want or need and showing them how to get it. Don't be salesy! Connect them to an outcome where they have solved their problem. The difference you make helps them see you as a solution provider and not someone looking to take advantage of them.

Credibility 101

As we make our way toward the finish line, we need to keep our eyes on the incredible components that make up a successful sales strategy.

The framework (ESP Method: Value-Service-Trust) is fueled by the process (Five Cs of Every Sales Experience: Care-Connect-Clarify-Confirm-Commit). When these components are expertly delivered to your client or your customer, you will establish the kind of credibility that gets you invited back. This is where you get to stay connected and remain in a position to offer more value in the future. Your credibility is up to you. When you move beyond the transaction and focus on serving your customer, your credibility goes up. Credibility is defined as the quality of being believable or worthy of trust. [41]

Bingo! If you want to be a person who is looked upon as believable and worthy of trust, serve others. Put their needs first and you will always win.

Handling Objections

I can't deny it. The topic of *handling objections* increases my enthusiasm for my job. I know it sounds a bit peculiar, but I really like the challenge of helping someone gain clarity in the ideas about which they have already made up their minds. There are times when these assumptions lead them to the incorrect conclusion. Let me give you an example.

I was attending a regional sales conference in Nashville, Tennessee, in the spring of 2017 with my colleagues from a national insurance company. We were working through an exercise about understanding our value proposition and addressing different ways to effectively handle objections. We were divided into groups and each table had two specific assignments to work through and then choose someone from the table to report to the entire group when called upon. I was sitting at a table with four people new to the company and one from a different department. Since I was the most experienced, they all asked me to stand up and report our findings to the group.

When our turn came to share what we came up with, I stood and reported on our table assignment. Then my boss, who was facilitating the discussion, asked me to remain standing and respond to the following question: "Jimmy, how would you respond when you are asking for more new business opportunities and your client says to you, 'You want what everyone else wants.'"

I paused, smiled, and said, "I love it when people say that to me! Here's how I typically respond to this objection."

I went on to explain that when I hear that objection I say, "Before we go any further, let's be clear about what you just said. I'm sure that you feel like everyone is asking you for the same type of business, but I'm not joining in and asking you to send me what everyone else wants. Three years ago, some of these carriers wouldn't even write these classes, and three years from now they may change their appetite again. What I'm asking for are target classes for our company. They have always been a big part of our appetite. This is our sweet spot! We're not asking for what everyone else wants, they are now asking for what we have *always* wanted. We are not a short-term solution for these classes of business. We are your long-term strategy for these target markets!" When I had finished, there was a burst of applause and a proud smile from my boss.

Over the years, I have worked hard at fielding all sorts of objections. My focus has been on clarifying what is really being said and either confirming, or refining the perspective of the person who offered the objection. You don't have to be afraid of what someone else is saying. It may simply be that they don't have all the facts and are simply repeating what one of your competitors said about your business.

One of the best ways to handle objections is to ask questions to clarify their statements. This strategy provides insight into their perspective. Don't be defensive. Be curious. It could be as simple as:

- Tell me more. What do you mean by that statement?

- What else have you heard?

- Is there more about this idea that you could share with me?

- In addition to that are there any other reasons why you won't consider what I have to offer?

- That's an interesting question and one that I hear often.

I could go on about all the ways to respond to an objection, but what I really want you to understand is there are many motivations that cause people to raise objections. Don't take it personally. Think of it as information or feedback. It's just part of the process.

Treat objections like basic questions. If you know the answer, respond with grace. No need to put anyone down for raising an objection. How you respond tells them something about you and your character. Keep this positive and appropriate. If you don't know the answer, don't fake it! Thank them for their question and commit to getting back to them with an answer. Make sure you follow through if you commit to respond back to them.

Follow Up and Follow Through – A Matched Set

As you read in chapters 9 and 10, the practice of confirming and committing to what happens next are essential components of the process. Please understand that the follow up and follow through are not mutually exclusive events. They are vitally connected—as matched set. They go together. As parts of the process, they include connection, motion, and commitment in bringing the desired value to your prospects and customers.

When it comes to selling, follow up and follow through happen both during the process *and* after the completion of the sale. It's how you deliver the products and services, and how you follow up to make sure they received all that they ordered. It's also in how you follow through in closing any and all loose ends. Make it a point to make yourself available to any questions or concerns they have after any deal is complete. This builds their confidence in you and affirms in their minds the decision they made to work with you.

Sales Perspective Habits

Start
- If how you finish matters, then spend the time to work on your final delivery.
- Strive to finish well.

Analyze
- Even at this phase overtalking can get ahold of you. Prepare to avoid it at all costs.

Learn
- Examine your past sales experiences and find the comfortable conclusions that leave your customers confident they are on the right track.

Engage
- Follow up and follow through are critical steps. Don't go silent after they've decided to keep working with you.

Serve
- Prove your worth to them by treating them well after a decision or transaction takes place.

PART THREE
YOUR NEW WORLD

HOW TO BE WELCOME ANYWHERE

BE PART OF THE SOLUTION

"You must have a good time meeting people if you expect them to have a good time meeting you." [42]
— Dale Carnegie

Words of Encouragement

WHAT DOES IT MEAN to encourage someone? What's the value of sharing encouragement with others? While some may look at it as a form of flattery or even false flattery, it usually is intended to lift someone up from their current state or affirm them in what they're doing. The definition of encourage is 1) *To inspire with courage, spirit, or hope: Hearten;* 2) *To spur on: Stimulate;* 3) *To give help or patronage to: Foster.* [43]

Many years ago, I was at a conference and during a break I found myself in conversation with some of the leaders at the event. I thanked them for inspiring us with their stories. They thanked me for the kind words and expressed the importance of sharing encouragement in the world as many people have unspoken challenges and need a little affirmation that they are seen and heard. It was in this setting that I heard the following words spoken back to me that have resonated in my soul ever since:

"The world belongs to the encourager!"

This is not about manipulating anyone in any way. From the point of sincerity, it's about acknowledging and affirming people right where they are. Over the years, I've learned the value of encouraging someone on their journey. I have also learned that when I need a little encouragement, if I focus on giving it away, it always finds its way back to me. Encouragement is a personal and invaluable way to connect with others. This point has its foundation in what we discussed in Chapter 7 regarding the process of building a bridge of influence. Your ultimate goal is to deliver value and solutions to your prospects and customers. They will buy into you when you are willing to share your heart with them.

Bring a Different Game

One day I had lunch with Eric Klein, an insurance agent with Assured Partners of Minnesota. We have developed a strong relationship in business, share a passion for guitars, and have become good friends. Our conversation revolved around a number of topics including helping guide some of the new agents in his office that he was mentoring. He shared how they were consistently stuck on their own perspective about the sales process. As he was describing some of their struggles, I was reminded of my own challenges when I was starting out in sales.

We went on to talk about some of the great relationships we had built with our past customers. Eric shared how he noticed that my focus on the customer's perspective was different from most of my competition. Eric went on to tell me that he sees many different company reps in his office. They all seem to have the same question for him and say, "What have you got for me? What are you working on that you can send my way?"

Eric smiled, looked directly at me, and said, "I've never heard you say those words to me. You are always interested in my customers and look for ways to help me serve them. You are not like everyone else that calls on me." He went on to share that my understanding of the customer's perspective has been impactful and effective in the ways I help him find the best solutions that serve his customers. We have written a lot of business together over the years and I have a tremendous amount of respect for Eric and for the way he engages his customers. We've made a good team in business because we align our hearts by keeping our focus on what's most important to the customer. Our approach in this matter is unified, which brings a unique blend of care and service to everyone we have the opportunity to work with.

As I drove home from that lunch meeting, I felt a keen sense of value from Eric's unsolicited affirmation. His heart to share how my different approach has had a positive impact on him, and his business relationships was a great gift to me.

You don't have to be like everyone else. You get to be your best self when you remember the importance of thinking through all the relationships in the sales experience and strive to consistently bring a positive impact to all of them.

First Impressions

Meeting new clients has consistently been one of the best parts of my job. A few years ago, as we were heading into the New Year, I was asked to take on some new responsibility by adding the state of Wisconsin to my territory. It's a border state and not that far of a stretch for me, as I lived twenty minutes from the border. I scheduled some agency visits, and my first stop was at an agency in the greater Milwaukee area where I met the owner and his commercial lines team.

After the initial introductions, I shared an overview of what I was going to cover in this meeting, but before we got to the agenda, I wanted to know if they had any initial questions or concerns that I should know about. This invitation caused the person who was sitting on my right, to turn to me and express her frustration with the lack of follow-up and response from home office when she called and left a message or emailed a question asking for a response. As is my typical practice, I turned to face her to let her know that she had my undivided attention as she shared her concerns. I apologized on behalf of my company and thanked her for her willingness to share this important feedback with me. I went on to share with her and with everyone that we have a new team that will be working with this agency going forward. I also let them know that they could call or email me, and I would reply to them within a day with an answer or update on the progress in getting their answers.

At the end of this meeting, I thanked everyone for the opportunity to meet with them and learn more about how I can help them grow. The person who had raised her concerns earlier in the meeting turned to me again and said she had a couple of additional questions for me. After saying goodbye and thanks to the rest of the group, I gave her my attention once again. After she asked her questions, I told her that I would investigate them and get back to her by the end of the day with an update. She thanked me and we said our good-byes.

Later that same day, I made a call to my home office partner, got an answer to her first question, and sent an email to my client with the update as promised. Here was her response to my email.

"Thanks so much for getting back to me on this, Jimmy! We all enjoyed meeting you too. Your energy about what you're doing is really refreshing and you gave us a clear picture of what we can expect from you and your company. Best of all, we now have a good idea of where you will really be able to shine for us!"

Her response encouraged me. When I hear things like, "Your energy about what you're doing is really refreshing..." I am reminded that they see a variety of company representatives that call on their office with a *"What have you got for me?"* attitude that conveys a different message. If you want to stand out from the crowd, you'll want to be consistent in not just telling, but showing people that you are there to serve them. Understand that when you communicate, you let them know what's most important to you by how you connect with them and clarify your message for their benefit. Don't be afraid to speak in ways that demonstrate your focus is on their customers and how you can help them win in the marketplace. You'll be surprised how that resonates with an organization. It's so different from what they typically experience, that you can find yourself standing out from your competition by approaching your dialogue with a focused perspective that keeps them thinking about how your products and services help *them* win with *their* customers. Everyone wants to win. When your clients recognize that you are there to help them do exactly that, they'll receive you and your message with open arms.

Notice that although I had an agenda for this meeting, I was willing to set it aside to address their questions or concerns first. This posture demonstrates where your focus is without you having to tell them directly. When I'm in a meeting with a group, especially when meeting them for the first time, I make it a habit to write their names down in the order of where they are each sitting in the room. That way I can respond to them by name when they ask a question or offer a perspective. This simple act on my part connects them to me quickly because I place an emphasis on the importance of knowing and remembering their names. This is also valuable at the end of the meeting when you're able to say goodbye and thank them by name for their time. Dale Carnegie says, "The most important sound to anyone is the sound of their own name." [44] According to Rachel Ingber, "A name represents identity, a deep feeling, and holds tremendous significance to its owner." [45] Make it a point to get good at the skill of remembering names. It can be a game-changer in developing your relationships, especially with those you are meeting for the first time.

The Turn Around

One day I was meeting with the team from one of my clients out in western Minnesota. I had my agenda of items I sent to them in advance to address in this meeting. Before we got started, the owner told me he had some things they needed to get to the bottom of right away. I set aside my agenda and asked him what was on his mind.

He proceeded to grill me about our service levels and the lack of follow-up from customer service when they do reach out for information. I listened intently as he and his team shared the agency's frustrations with what they hoped was not going to be a regular pattern going forward. Once they had asked all their questions, I asked if there was anything else they were concerned about. They told me that was it and I proceeded to address them one by one. As I covered each topic, I asked clarifying questions to make sure I understood their concerns properly. I continued this pattern throughout the list of questions and with each response I took the opportunity to provide context about what's happened, what we are doing about it, what I will do about it, and how things are designed to improve going forward.

They listened and asked additional questions of me as well. After addressing their questions and concerns, it was amazing how the tone in the meeting lightened up. They voiced their concerns to a listening ear and heard acknowledgement about those concerns. *(Remember, this is the time to listen with the intent to understand, not the time to push back or dispute their concerns.)*

Once we were able to move on, I shared some of the areas where we are having our greatest success, thus bringing opportunities for growth to their agency. We switched from covering concerns to pre-qualifying new business opportunities.

As our meeting was wrapping up, the owner sat back in his chair and said, "I like the way you do business!" He went on to thank me for handling and owning the concerns they shared, and for understanding and showing them where the opportunities lie for future growth. It was clear that he could tell I was there to help *them* grow *their* business.

Be Part of the Solution

When you are recognized as a solution provider—as someone who adds value to others and is concerned with what's most important to them—you will always be welcome wherever you go. Your heart of service will open doors for you that are often closed to others.

Referrals are the result of you gaining someone else's trust. Before anyone gives you a referral, they need you to "put a ribbon on the box." This is the way I often refer to the process for finishing the sales process all the way to the end.

Let me give you an example. Have you ever received a gift for your birthday or holiday where the gift is given to you unwrapped and still in the bag from the store where it was purchased? How does that make you feel? Special? Unimportant? An after-thought? Do you feel valued by the giver or simply a last-minute thought to a forgotten occasion?

On the other hand, when you receive a beautifully wrapped gift with a bright ribbon around it, does that make you feel special? Do you feel recognized and valued by the giver? Are you excited about the gift they chose especially for you?

Which type of gift makes you feel like you're seen or held in high regard in the eyes of the giver? The key to being part of the solution is your effort to recognize the value of the people you are working with and the solution you are ultimately providing.

The Power of a Smile

As we learned in Chapter 6, presenting yourself well to your customers starts before you are face-to-face. However, when the time comes to finally meet, your attitude and expression rule the moment. A smile can make such an amazing difference in creating a welcoming bond with your new connection.

Moving beyond your general appearance, your facial expression followed by your words have the greatest impact on the start of your relationship. According to Karyn Hall, PhD, "Smiling is contagious. When you give a warm and friendly smile, often others will smile back. You get a moment of feeling connected and accepted, as you spread happiness." Hall goes on to say, "Smiling signals to others that you are friendly and likable and not a threat. You improve the impression you make on others, and you come across as more likable. They will want to be around you and see you as more competent. And you will tend to be more productive and creative. Amazing. Smiling leads others to see you as more trustworthy. When you smile, you are signaling that you are open and friendly." [46]

If you want to be welcome anywhere, don't forget to notify your face! Remember, it's not just one thing you do that makes the difference between you and your competition. It's the entire package of who you are, how you connect, and how you consistently make others feel valued.

Sales Perspective Habits

Start
- Review the times in your career that you served someone, and it caused them to regularly welcome you into their office.

Analyze
- How has your service of others opened doors for you?
- Think of the people you look forward to spending time with. What do they do that makes you always willing to welcome them into your life?

Learn
- Learn to ask them the "Highest and Best Way" they would like to engage with you.
- Listen for their answers and follow through as they suggest.

Engage
- Bring your energy and enthusiasm to every visit. Be sincere and authentic.

Serve
- When they see you are there for them, they'll want to make sure to include you in any upcoming events or opportunities to add value to their team.

BUILD LASTING RELATIONSHIPS
PEOPLE MATTER MOST

> *"Trust is the glue of life. It's the most essential ingredient in effective communication. It's the foundational principle that holds all relationships."*[47]
> — Stephen R. Covey

An Invaluable Lesson in Relationships

"LIFE'S A PEOPLE BUSINESS. You have to figure out how to work well and get along with others." These words from my dad have had a profound impact on my career and my perspective on the importance of relationships. I had the privilege of working alongside my father in his business for 17 years. I observed how he connected with people. I watched as he welcomed people and put them at ease and when called upon, how he handled demanding situations and difficult people. He demonstrated the importance of recognizing the value in the other person, even when they chose to be difficult. I watched as he won them over by how he consistently treated them with respect and kindness, even when they didn't return the favor. His consistent pattern of serving and honoring others was a great gift to me.

There was a time when we discussed this topic more specifically and he shared his life philosophy about why it's important to treat the customer well all the time. He'd say things like, "The customer is always right. Even when they're wrong, you treat them well. Even when you'd love to tell them how wrong they really are, you don't do it!" In all honesty, I must admit, in my early days in business, I was more likely to correct someone who was wrong, especially when they were being unreasonable. My dad would go on to say, "You don't want to win the battle and lose the war." I asked him what he meant by that statement. He clarified by helping me see the importance of not putting someone in their place when they're wrong. He would much rather have me give them a level of respect, even when I didn't think they deserved it. This would help me remain on the high road of kindness to others.

He said, "If you insist on showing disrespect toward your prospect or customer, they will leave and go tell 10 to 15 of their friends how poorly you treated them, and you'll never know it. You'll also never have the opportunity for those 10 to 15 people to be your customers!"

BOOM! That resonated across my brain in a way that I had never considered. The deeper meanings of building quality relationships through trust and respect have guided me throughout my career. Does it mean I no longer make mistakes in building relationships? No. It simply means that when I do make a mistake, I know how to re-center my mind and review with discernment, honesty, and humility where I screwed up. This allows me to make things right by owning my behavior and seeking reconciliation with my customer.

Don't take for granted the importance of owning your behavior. When you have wronged someone, even if they haven't said anything to you, and you take the time to be honest with yourself, I encourage you to take the opportunity to acknowledge the error and offer to make things right. People will respect you for owning your behavior. They will also ultimately respect you when you take their verbal frustration without fighting back. This is a great opportunity for you to manage yourself in difficult situations. When a challenge arises, I often shift my focus to the possibilities of a new outcome. In other words, I start seeing challenges as opportunities. Let me share a unique story from early in my career in sales.

Take the Heat and Don't Get Burned

I've had the distinct "privilege" of being yelled at on many occasions in my life, with most of them coming during the years that I worked for my dad's building supply company. Now, I wasn't yelled at by my father much, it was mostly when a construction foreman was sitting at the jobsite with a phone in his hand acting important and tough in front of his workers as he yelled to get what he wanted. This most often involved his frustration that his delivery wasn't there when his workers showed up and he had to answer his boss as to why he had workers getting paid to stand around doing nothing! This was costing his boss money, and nobody was happy.

I came to learn that all the yelling they were doing wasn't personal, it was just business. There were a few people in my dad's office who hated dealing with these guys because all they did was yell, and they were rude and no fun to deal with. Of course, that meant that I was the one who got to take it from them, and I learned the importance of consistently doing the following:

1. Listening to their plight

2. Letting them blow off some steam

3. Setting out to solve their problem to the very best of my ability.

I also learned the importance of controlling my emotions and gained a deeper understanding of the importance of what you say and when you say it—or *don't* say it!

Years later I was in sales as a territory manager for a national insurance company. My clients were independent insurance agents who represented our product to their customers. The skills I learned in taking the heat and not getting burned came in real handy one Friday afternoon in June. My family and I were going to be heading to family camp for the weekend. Earlier in the day I had received a call from one of my new clients telling me that he wanted to place a large order with me. After reviewing all the details of making this work and getting approval from my regional underwriter, I confirmed that we would work with his team to complete the deal, and I thanked him for his business. It's 10:00 am and everyone is happy.

An hour went by, and I got a phone call from the underwriting manager that there was a problem with making this deal happen. There were several factors that hadn't come up earlier that made the manager uneasy about this account and the potential negative impact this account could have on our territory's loss ratio. (OK, I know, I know, too much detail. Just hang in there for another minute as this is about to get exciting!)

All the reasons I heard didn't solve the problem that I had going back to the agent and telling him that upon further review, management was now rejecting the plan to move the business to our territory. I was directed to call him and tell him the deal was off. I needed time to think about this.

"It's time to load the van!" Those words from my wife broke me out of the fog I was in, trying to figure out how to help this guy win when I was about to cause him to lose. "Be right there," was all I could say as I made my way out of my office to begin the loading process for family camp while still highly distracted by what I needed to do next with this agent. I got the van loaded up in short order and called my direct boss to walk through my options. He was in the same office as the underwriting manager and was going to go discuss it further and call me back. I felt a little relieved that I was getting some assistance with a tough circumstance as I had only been with my company for 10 months.

When my boss called back, he shared his conversation with the underwriting manager and ended up confirming the decision as "One of those unusual circumstances that rarely happen." Not a great comfort to know that I was also becoming the odd circumstance or the exception guy in my territory. Maybe that's just because I learned from my dad the importance of fighting for my customers and trying to solve their problems to the best of my ability.

With the confirmation that there was nothing else I could do to change the outcome, I decided to make the phone call. I was greeted by a warm, "What's up?" from the agent. I told him that I had received news from management that the deal we spoke of earlier was off and that management did not want his request to be processed. It was denied. His immediate reaction and tone changed. The words he said to me I cannot repeat here. His choice of words, what he said, and what he called me crossed virtually everyone's line. He had already put everything in motion and told his customer that he was moving their account over to my company based on our conversation from earlier in the morning. He demanded to know why and who he could talk to about it. I told him the specific reasons why and that I had already talked to my boss and two other managers about this issue, and that this decision came directly from them. He said a few additional choice words and hung up the phone.

Well, that wasn't great, but I got the message delivered. It was time to leave for camp and my phone rang. I asked my wife to drive as this was going to need my attention for a little bit. It was my boss and the underwriting manager on a conference call wanting to know how the call went. I told them that he didn't take it well, even after I explained to him the reasons they had provided. I asked for more clarification and then put my boss and the underwriter in my agent's shoes and asked them to try and understand this issue and the reasons for the denial from his perspective. If nothing else, it helped me get them to see an additional perspective on their decision.

My phone was buzzing. It was the agent. I told them I had to go, and I would call back. My agent was really struggling with the reasoning for the decision and went on to tell me how wrong I was, and that my company's decision was unjust, improper, and a few other words I won't include here. Still steaming, he wanted to know if there was any chance that this could be remedied before the day was out.

He asked me to take some additional information to my bosses and see if they would be willing to still complete this deal. I told him that I would make a call and get back to him shortly.

Back on the phone with my boss I told him what had happened on the call and although the agent had clarified things from his perspective, it wasn't enough to change the outcome. I let my boss know that even though I was a little frustrated with the decision we made, I was on the side of my team and was going to maintain our company's position on this decision.

I called the agent back and told him that the information brought hadn't changed the circumstances or the decision from management and that this deal was not going to happen today. Surprisingly, by now he seemed frustrated but not mean. It was as if he was getting his arms around his limited options at this stage in the day. He thanked me for trying and said that he was going to see if he could get everything put back together the way it was previously for his customer. He also thanked me for fighting for him.

I hung up the phone and felt a little better. I looked over at my wife who was amazed at what she had just witnessed, and how

I wrestled with this issue and fought for all the information so I could help my agent out and keep my integrity, even when he was willing to throw his out! I finally started to relax and just let my wife drive as I engaged my two sons who were in the back of the van.

It wasn't long after that when my phone rang again. It was the agent, and he sounded different, subdued, and very direct. He said, "Jimmy, I want you to know something. I am sorry for what I said earlier today and I'm very sorry for the things I said to you and about you. I was angry at the decision, and I took it out on you. I'm very sorry." I told him it was all right. I knew that he was upset and that he was just trying to take care of his customer. Then he said, "One more thing. I want you to know that I noticed something very specific about you and it has had a great impact on me. When I was yelling at you and saying the nasty things that I said, you just took it. You didn't yell back. You didn't hang up. You just took it. I want you to know that I am impressed by that, and it has told me so much about your character and I have shown you how mine pales in comparison. I thank you for the way you handled this situation. I could tell that you were fighting for me and that's all I can ever ask of you. You were the man today. I know your handle is Jimmy Z but from now on I'm going to call you Z-Dog! I think we are going to be great friends! Call me next week and we'll get together."

Did that just happen? I was surprised and pleased and grateful for his reaction. I was grateful to my dad for all he had taught me about how to handle the customer. Treating the customer with respect and working with them when they are frustrated, angry, and even wrong in their response can still allow them to ultimately win.

From my dad, I've learned the importance of helping the customer win. I have found over the years that a truly successful Win-Win happens when I take my eyes off myself and put them on my customer and do everything I can to help them win!

If you and I do that, then eventually we will win. We will win in gained confidence, trust, respect, friendship, and more business. We might even get a cool nickname out of it. But we need to earn the relationship first—that's what makes the business really mean something.

I turned to my wife and kids and told them what the agent had just said to me. Then I told my sons, "Life is a people business, boys. You must learn how to handle all kinds of circumstances and deal fairly with people even when they are unwilling to deal fairly with you. People who sell houses always talk about the three keys in real estate: Location, Location, Location. Well in life the three keys are: *Relationships, Relationships, Relationships.* You must be able to work with all kinds of people and you will do well if you strive to add value to their lives and treat them well in all circumstances."

My dad taught me how to treat people right even when they are wrong or upset or when the circumstances are out of your control. Taking the other person's perspective will always help you treat them well and demonstrate that you are striving to help *them* win.

Two and a half hours later it was time to exhale. And stop for dinner.

Z-Dog was hungry!

Trust Is the Cornerstone of Relationships

This may come as a surprise to you, but in sales, people matter way more than products or services. You build trust by serving them, not by selling them. As we learned in Chapter 2, regarding the importance of *Redefining WIN-WIN*, when your focus is on helping someone else win first, you earn the opportunity to gain their trust.

Another place to build trust is found in an honest approach in all areas of your business and your life. According to Charles Causey, in his book, CANDOR, we learn a strategic game plan for building a methodology of clear communication. Causey provides a guiding definition of candor to help us understand its importance in valued communication. "Candor is the quality of being forthright, honest, and sincere. It can be a highly effective tool to shape our spheres of influence. How does it work? Candor sheds light on a situation, allowing important issues to be discovered. As a surgeon needs good light to see the operation he may be performing, important discussions need candor to find the truth." He goes on to point out an amazing truth about how candor can help individuals and organizations progress to new heights. Causey says, "Candor will not only help the organizations we serve, it will sharpen us as individuals. If we allow others to be candid with us—and in the process become conduits for receiving feedback—it will take us to places of trust and loyalty we never thought possible." [48]

Sales Perspective Habits

Start
- Read books on sales and people skills (see suggested reading in the back of the book).

Analyze
- Learn from the experts, both past and present, on relationship selling.
- Find the tools that can help specific parts of your process.

Learn
- Turn all learning into your own voice and style. Don't get caught up copying someone else.
- Be your authentic self.

Engage
- Life is truly a people business. Be your best self in every experience.

Serve
- Enjoy doing business with them and they'll enjoy doing business with you.

THE BIG PICTURE

YOUR SALES LEGACY

"Legacy is not leaving something for people. It's leaving something in people." [49]

— Peter Strople

Your Sales/Life Compass

To periodically check my bearings and make sure that I'm moving in my intended direction, I ask myself the following questions:

Where are you going?
Are you on track?
Is this moving you toward your goals?
Are you sure this is what you want?
Are there any alternatives you should consider?

Is this the best you can do or is there more for you to give?

How is your purpose impacted by the trajectory you are on?

Of course, I could go on and on with questions about what I'm doing and where I'm going. The purpose of this exercise is not to challenge what I'm doing, but rather, to pull out my mental compass and make sure I am on track based on what I value the most.

To accurately answer these questions, I must first identify what's most important to me. Like a compass helps us know what direction we're heading and whether we're on course, having a set of guiding principles provides the basis from which we measure our direction and progress. Throughout my career in sales, I have learned that the more I make my key decisions around life principles, the easier it is to remain consistent with my character, my responses, and my engagement, whether I'm at work or at home. I remind myself that my situation should not reflect a different me. It's important that my character shows itself dependable in all circumstances. This is why I live by a set of guiding principles that carry over into all areas of my life. They are essential to how I conduct myself in my sales career and they help guide me in my personal life as well.

Your Top Ten Guiding Principles

Success isn't luck or available just for a few. The foundation of successfully navigating business careers and life is often found in the non-negotiables or the guiding principles that people who want to be the best in their field adhere to throughout their journey. This is not career driven only, as the principles are an essential part of the individual's makeup and flow in both their career path and their personal path.

In the case of business, we often look to those who've gone before us as successful leaders and successful communicators. These are the people we want to learn more from, to mentor us, to guide us, and to share with us the principles that helped them accomplish what they've accomplished. We look up to them, we admire them, and we want to learn from their journey.

We can observe a similar model when we spin over to the world of sports or entertainment. A particular player in a sport will have a group of coaches, trainers, etc., all invited to help these individuals accelerate their growth. For example, in golf, you might have a coach who helps you with the fundamentals and execution of your swing, a trainer who helps you get physically fit, and a sports psychologist, who helps you get mentally fit. Each of these individuals help you strive to be better and play your absolute best. This coaching and training will help you in all circumstances, including days when you're feeling good and everything clicks, and on days when nothing seems to be working as it should. Regardless of the day, what will keep you centered is a set of standards or guiding principles. Will you feel your best every day? No. Will you do your best every day? That's up to you. What motivates most people is adhering to a set of standards or principles—your fundamentals for life. You might even repeat these statements to yourself on a regular basis: *This is who I am. This is how I will respond to adversity. This is how I will respond to success. This is how I will remain consistent over time in business and in life.*

In sales, we often look to those who are successful at connecting, communicating, handling objections, and driving results. If I'm a business leader or a business owner, I will not focus solely on how I manage my people. My goal should be to effectively communicate what the vision of the organization is and how to get my entire organization on the same page about where we're going and what we're striving to accomplish. Finding good people, keeping good people, and providing opportunities for them to grow personally and professionally is what great leaders do. Great leaders are driven daily not necessarily by a "To Do" list, but more often by a list of guiding principles. Let me give you some examples.

As a young man, Benjamin Franklin, struggled with interpersonal communication. He was often thought of as a selfish, intellectual bully by the very nature of how he criticized others in public. After receiving some critical feedback from a trusted advisor, Franklin sought to change his ways. He crafted a specific list of virtues that he pursued in his daily habits. These led him to eventually be regarded as a man of influence among his peers. Here are the list of his virtues and a glimpse into his mindset as to their importance.

13 Virtues of Benjamin Franklin – The Autobiography of Benjamin Franklin

1. TEMPEREANCE. Eat not to dullness; drink not to elevation.

2. SILENCE. Speak not but what may benefit others or yourself; avoid trifling conversation.

3. ORDER. Let all your things have their places; let each part of your business have it's time.

4. RESOLUTION. Resolve to perform what you ought; perform without fail what you resolve.

5. FRUGALITY. Make no expense but to do good to others or yourself; i.e., waste nothing.

6. INDUSTRY. Lose no time: be always employ'd in something useful: cut off all unnecessary actions.

7. SINCERITY. Use no hurtful deceit; think innocently and justly, and, if you speak, speak accordingly.

8. JUSTICE. Wrong no one by doing injuries, or omitting the benefits that are your duty.

9. MODERATION. Avoid extremes; forbear resenting injuries so much as you think they deserve.

10. CLEANLINESS. Tolerate no uncleanliness in body, cloaths, or habitation.

11. TRANQUILLITY. Be not disturbed at trifles, or at accidents common or unavoidable.

12. CHASTITY. Rarely use veneery but for health or offspring, never to dullness, weakness, or the injury of your own or another's peace or reputation.

13. HUMILITY. Imitate Jesus and Socrates.

As for how to acquire these virtues, Franklin advised: "My intention being to acquire the habitude of all these virtues, I'd judged it would be well not to distract my attention by attempting the whole at once, but to fix it on one of them at a time; and, when I should be master of that, then to proceed to another, and so on, till I should have gone thro' the thirteen; and, as the previous acquisition of some might facilitate the acquisition of certain others, I arrang'd with that view, as they stand above." [50]

Don't let his old English throw you. His strategy can guide you to build a depth of character that doesn't come naturally, but by intention and daily commitment.

Legendary NCAA Basketball coach John Wooden died in 2010, but his legacy remains as powerful as ever. He was known for his remarkable record where from 1964 through 1975, his UCLA basketball teams won 10 NCAA championships, including streaks of seven consecutive titles, 88 straight regular season victories, and 38 straight NCAA tournament wins. As a young boy, he was given a gift by his father that caused John to pursue life with a seven-point creed that defined how he carried himself and also showed in his commitment to pass these traits along to others throughout his life.

Seven Point Creed – A Philosophy of Life, John Wooden, Legendary Basketball Coach

1. Be true to yourself.

2. Help others.

3. Make each day your masterpiece.

4. Drink deeply from good books, especially the Bible.

5. Make friendship a fine art.

6. Build a shelter against a rainy day.

7. Pray for guidance and count and give thanks for your blessings every day. [51]

Dr. Bob Rotella, in his book *Make Your Next Shot Your Best Shot*, shares the Top Ten lists of some successful champions in sports, business, and life. Rotella says, "Strive to better yourself in all areas of life, not just in your business or career." [52] These words ring clear when you realize that you are more than what you do for work. Who you are as a person should be consistent across all areas of your life.

This reference to identifying or compiling a Top Ten was common among late-night television hosts or champions from sports or business. Whether it was Jack Nicklaus or Tiger Woods, Michael Jordan or Kobe Bryant, coaches John Wooden or Vince Lombardi, or the number of late-night TV personalities that shared a countdown on a random list of topics, the ranking lists of goals, or priorities was commonplace in these areas. Of course, we can embrace this strategy from the business world with John C. Maxwell's *The 21 Irrefutable Laws of Leadership* or Stephen R. Covey's *The 7 Habits of Highly Effective People,* just to name a couple. Most books written about sales have a process or procedure to follow to close the deal or win the sale, or as you've already discovered in this book where I share the *Five Cs of Every Sales Experience*, to help you transform the value you provide, the service you deliver and the trust you build with every customer.

The idea of listing or ranking the important components to guide me in business and in life challenged me to examine how I conduct myself and how I would identify my own primary guidelines. I wanted to look at both business and personal perspectives and motives, as I recognized the importance of not holding on to double standards or acting differently depending on my circumstance or setting.

When you look at Jimmy Z's Top Ten Guiding Principles, keep in mind that you want to identify the most important principles for your own life. Feel free to use this as an example or to spark the words that ring true for your approach to life. Use language that closely relates to your mindset. Your ability to be consistent throughout your life starts when you identify what's most important to you as you navigate each and every day.

I wish I could tell you that I have always been the same person at work as at home. Unfortunately, that's not always been the case. I'm not proud of that. I look back at times in my life when I was more focused on my career than I was on my family. I am striving every day to elevate the narrative of my life, not just my career.

Hanging around people of character who have been willing to mentor me to be my best in all areas of life has helped me embrace my shortcomings and cause me to focus on living with a consistent pattern of character. Through my team of mentors, my personal Board of Directors, that I wrote about in my book PEAK PERSPECTIVE, I have learned the importance of having structure, character, integrity, and trust throughout my life. Having a set of guiding principles has helped me understand the importance of my character development and my reputation at home and at work.

As you read earlier in Chapter 4, I believe that selling is serving. I have found that if I want that to be true at work, it must be true throughout my life. If selling is serving, the impact I have on the people I serve should be guided by the same principles I engage in other areas of my life. The consistency of character is a high calling! Here are my Top Ten Guiding Principles:

Jimmy Z's Top Ten Guiding Principles – for work and life:

1. Be Enthusiastic

2. Be Curious

3. Be Consistent in Character – Live Out My Faith

4. Focus on Others – Encourage Them / Stand for Them

5. Be Present Where I Am

6. Operate With Integrity

7. Keep My Cool / Remain Calm

8. Learn From Success & Failure

9. Remain Humble

10. Have Fun

Each of these principles has specific meaning and depth for me. They help keep me on track in living my life. What's most important to me may not be the same for you. That is why I encourage you to make your own list. When you begin to think about your own guiding principles, expand your thinking beyond your career. Your reputation should be built across all areas of your life. This strategy protects you from being one type of person at work, another in your community, and another at home. Always strive to be the same person with the same personality and character wherever you are. Here is your opportunity to identify and list the guiding principles that you are already using or want to strive to make part of your own life.

My influence has come from many people who I have learned from by hearing them speak, reading their books, attending their conferences, or mentoring one-on-one: John C. Maxwell, Dr. Henry Cloud, Kary Oberbrunner, B. Joseph Pine, David Schaefer, John Zugschwert, Andy Garner, Ken Clarke, Dr. Denny Conroy, Dr. Tony Colson, Grant Baldwin, Donald Miller, Vince Miller, Jim Collins, Patrick Lencioni, Simon Sinek, David Horsager, Dale Carnegie, Frank Bettger, Norman Vincent Peale, Mike Weinberg, Susan A. Lund, Brian Dixon, Mike Kim, Rachel Pedersen, Niccie Kliegl, Daphne Jo Vought, Mark Leblanc, Kit Welchlin, Michael Hyatt, Lt. Col. Rob "Waldo" Waldman, Steven R. Covey, Tony Robbins, Dean Graziosi, Paul Batz, Geno Wickman, Jim Akers, Cardiff D. Hall, Jonathan Milligan, Mark Schinnerer, Oswald Chambers, Gary Chapman, J. Oswald Sanders, Timothy Keller, Robert Lewis, David Cottrell, Seth Godin, Dan Sullivan, Jon Giganti, James Clear, Mark LaChance, Chris Anderson, Jon

Acuff, Kindra Hall, Charles Causey, Dan Miller, Jeff Henderson, and the list goes on and on...

Craft Your Top Ten Guiding Principles

Start by thinking of the internal and external characteristics you want to consistently display in all areas of your life. Let my list above or a list from one your favorite champions in sports or business, help get your mind started on making your list. Remember to keep this about you and how you want to impact others in a positive way. Focus on how you'll add value to them by how you treat them. The best-case scenario is when these guidelines are woven together and become your standard operating procedure in all areas of your life. Let this first list be a starting point that can be refined and updated as you live your life. Recognize when and where you are consistent and where you need to increase your efforts in business or in life to gain consistency.

Take the time to review your thoughts and make your own list. Start by listing what's important to you. It might be easier to get your list down on paper first and then prioritize them. Go ahead and make your first draft in the following space:

My Top Ten Guiding Principles for Work and Life

1. _____

2. _____

3. _____

4. _____

5. _____

6. _____

7. _____

8. _____

9. _____

10. _____

I encourage you to take this list and share it with your mentors. Get their input and feedback. With this added perspective, you can refine and clarify all that's most important to you as you pursue adding value in your sales career and to everyone you encounter.

Sales Perspective Habits

Start
- Set out to establish your own list of guiding principles and live them out!

Analyze
- Review the examples in this chapter and pursue character traits from other books, articles, podcasts, etc.

Learn
- Learn how champions keep their focus on the finish line and build your mindset to match.

Engage
- Use the road map you lay out with your guiding principles and live them out with passion.

Serve
- Selling is serving. Enjoy the journey of blessing others each day and you will consistently add value to the lives of others.

APPENDIX

THE SALES PERSPECTIVE GAME PLAN

YOUR SALES STRATEGY

Putting It All Together

In this book, I have introduced the Essential Selling Perspective (ESP) Method containing the framework and system to elevate your sales impact to new heights. This method not only provides structure to your approach of adding value to your prospects and customers, it also uncovers the steps that deliver consistent connections to build lasting relationships. Understanding how to deliver Value, Service, and Trust to your prospects and customers, is the result of following the FIVE Cs of Every Sales Experience. Embrace this plan as your own by customizing it to your own style while keeping your customer's perspective paramount in your mind. This refined way of thinking will connect you to your prospects and customers in ways you could not achieve with a transaction mindset.

Essential Selling Perspective Method

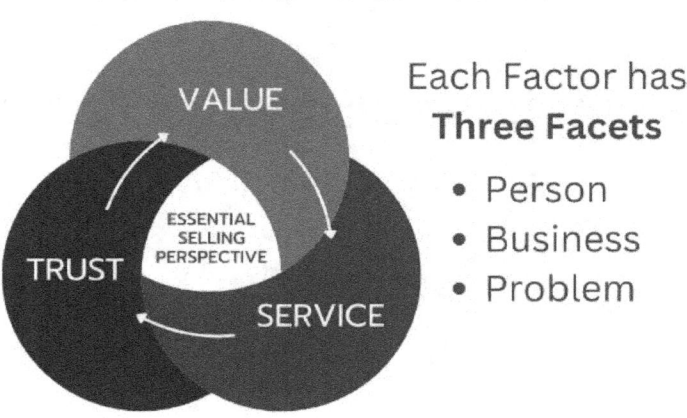

Five Cs of Every Sales Experience

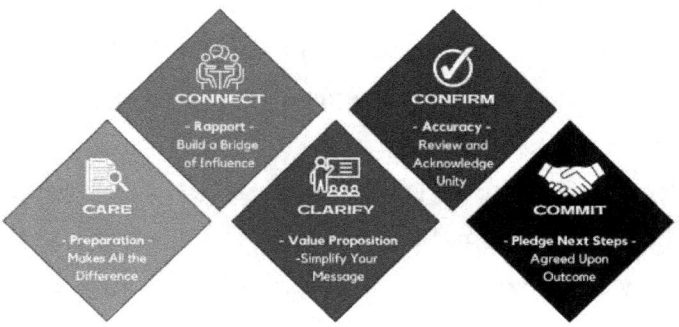

Scan / Click the QR Code below to access *Your Next Step* of The Sales Perspective Game Plan where you'll find a workbook containing highlights from each chapter, with a deeper dive into applying the lessons learned and incorporating them into your daily routine.

You can also access additional resources by visiting jimmyzspeaks.com/salesperspective.

THE SALES PERSPECTIVE READING PLAN

Recommended Reading

Winning With People, John C. Maxwell
The Experience Economy, B. Joseph Pine & James Gilmore
Atomic Habits, James Clear
The E Mind, Kary Oberbrunner
Know What You're FOR, Jeff Henderson
Stories That Stick, Kindra Hall
Integrity, Dr. Henry Cloud
The Only Sales Guide You'll Ever Need, Anthony Iannarino
Changing the Sales Conversation, Linda Richardson
High-Profit Prospecting, Mark Hunter
Candor, Charles Causey
The Thinking Advantage, Jill Young

The 4 Disciplines of Execution,
  Chris McChesney, Sean Covey, Jim Huling
Smarter, Faster, Better, Charles Duhigg
Deal-Storming, Tim Saunders
The Best Damn Sales Book Ever, Warren Greshes
Grow Your Business, Mark Leblanc
Start With Your People, Brian Dixon
New Sales Simplified, Mark Weinberg
How to Win Friends and Influence People, Dale Carnegie
How I Raised Myself From Failure to Success in Selling,
  Frank Bettger

ABOUT THE AUTHOR

Jimmy Zugschwert is an award-winning speaker, author, sales coach & trainer with a heart to help others climb to new heights in business and in life. As CEO of Summit Perspective, he specializes in training and leading individuals and organizations to grow their impact through a fresh perspective on connecting with their customers. With over four decades of sales experience and consistent production growth, Jimmy Z, will help your team convert ideas and strategies into tangible results through a simple shift in your perspective.

Jimmy enjoys golf – both playing and teaching, is an accomplished guitarist, and loves to read, study, and write to inspire others to live a life worth leaving. He lives in Minnesota with his wife, Nancy, where they have raised four sons. To have Jimmy Z share his engaging story through keynotes, break-out sessions, or workshops by bringing his **Sales Perspective** methodology to your business, team, or organization, you can contact him directly through his website at JIMMYZSpeaks.com.

CONNECT WITH JIMMY Z

JIMMY ZUGSCHWERT

SPEAKER
AUTHOR
SALES COACH
CONSULTANT

Follow him on your favorite social media platforms today

JIMMYZSpeaks.com

Mentorship | Sales | Leadership | Legacy | Faith | Marriage

Keynotes, Workshops, Online Courses, Masterminds, 1-on-1 Coaching

Learn more at JIMMYZSpeaks.com

Endnotes

1. Kary Oberbrunner, *The E Mind,* (Ethos Collective, Powell, OH, 2023)

2. Doug Baldwin, (http://www.brainyquote.com accessed July 2023)

3. Merriam-Webster Dictionary, (http://www.merriam-webster.com accessed July 2023)

4. Jeff Henderson, *Know What You're FOR*, (Zondervan Grand Rapids, MI, 2019)

5. Les Brown (http://www.brainyquotes.com, accessed July 2023)

6. Dale Carnegie, *How to Win Friends and Influence People*, (Pocket Books, New York, NY, 1936)

7. Bob Phibbs, (http://www.brainyquote.com, accessed July2023)

8. Linda Richardson, *Changing the Sales Conversation*, (McGraw-Hill Education, New York, NY 2014)

9. Merriam-Webster Dictionary, (http://www.merriam-webster.com, accessed July 2023)

10. Brian Tracy, (http://www.brainyquote.com, accessed July2023)

11. Glengarry Glen Ross, (http://www.imdb.com, Movie by David Mamet, 1992)

12. William A. Ward, (http://www.brainyquote.com, accessed July2023)

13. Merriam-Webster Dictionary, (http://www.merriam-webster.com, accessed July 2023)

14. B. Joseph Pine & James Gilmore, *The Experience Economy*, (Harvard Business Review Press, Boston, MA, 2020)

15. Most often attributed to Theodore Roosevelt, (http://www.brainyquote.com, accessed July2023)

16. Benjamin Franklin, (http://www.brainyquote.com, accessed July2023)

17. Stephen Keague, *The Little Red Handbook of Public Speaking and Presenting,* (CreateSpace Independent Publishing Platform, 2012)

18. Robert Cialdini, *PRE-SUASION*, (Simon & Schuster Paperbacks, New York, NY, 2016)

19. Albert Einstein, (http://www.brainyquote.com, accessed July2023)

20. Merriam-Webster Dictionary, (http://www.merriam-webster.com accessed July2023)

21. Stephen R. Covey, *The 7 Habits of Highly Effective People* (Fireside, Simon & Schuster Bldg., Rockefeller Center, 1230 Avenue of the Americas, New York, New York, 10020, 1989)

22. Kary Oberbrunner, *Day Job to Dream Job*, (Ethos Collective, Powell, OH, 2018)

23. Harvard Office of Career Services, (https://careerservices.fas.harvard.edu/blog/2022/10/11/22, accessed July2023)

24. Dictionary.com (http://www.dictionary.com, accessed July2023)

25. Kary Oberbrunner, *Day Job to Dream Job*, (Ethos Collective, Powell, OH, 2018)

26. Frank Bettger, *How I Raised Myself From Failure to Success in Selling*, (Fireside/Prentice Hall, New York, NY, 1947, 1992)

27. Frank Bettger, *How I Raised Myself From Failure to Success in Selling*, (Fireside/Prentice Hall, New York, NY, 1947, 1992)

28. Merriam-Webster Dictionary, (http://www.merrian-webster.com, accessed July2023)

29. Stephen R. Covey, *The 7 Habits of Highly Effective People,* (Simon & Schuster, New York, NY, 1989)

30. Kindra Hall, *Stories That Stick,* (HarperCollins Leadership, New York, NY, 2019)

31. Frank Bettger, *How I Raised Myself From Failure to Success in Selling*, (Fireside/Prentice Hall, New York, NY, 1947,1992)

32. Zig Ziglar, (http://www.brainyquote.com, accessed July 2023)

33. Dictionary.com (http://www.dictionary.com accessed July2023)

34. Anthony Iannarino, *The Only Sales Guide You'll Ever Need*, (Penguin Random House, New York, NY, 2016)

35. Meb Keflezighi, Run to Overcome: The Inspiring Story of an American Champion's Long-Distance Quest to Achieve a Big Dream, Pg. 176, (Tyndale House Publishers, 2010, http://www.inspiringquotes.com, accessed July2023)

36. Heather Dorniden, (http://www.elitereaders.com/heatherdorniden, by Mark Andrew, Aug. 3, 2015)

37. YouTube, Heather Dorniden Wins the Race, (*https://www.youtube.com/watch?v=g9rUUz8cMDM*)

38. Merriam-Webster Dictionary, (http://www.merriam-webster.com accessed July2023)

39. Dr. Henry Cloud, *Integrity*, (HarperCollins Publishers, New York, NY, 2006)

40. Jeff Henderson, *Know What You're FOR*, (Zondervan, Grand Rapids, MI, 2019)

41. Dictionary.com, (http://www.dictionary.com accessed July2023)

42. Dale Carnegie, *How to Win Friends and Influence People*, (Pocket Books, New York, NY, 1936)

43. Dictionary.com (http://www.dictionary.com accessed July 2023)

44. Dale Carnegie, *How to Win Friends and Influence People*, (Pocket Books, New York, NY 1936)

45. Rachel Ingber, (http://www.kidadl.com accessed February 2024)

46. Karyn Hall, PhD, *The Importance of Smiling*, (http://www.psychcentral.com, March 2018)

47. Stephen R. Covey, (http://www.brainyquotes.com, accessed July2023)

48. Charles Causey, *Candor*, Northfield Publishing, Chicago, IL, 2021)

49. Peter Strople, (http://www.brainyquotes.com accessed July 2023)

50. Benjamin Franklin, *13 Virtues – The Autobiography of Benjamin Franklin*, (*www.goodreads.com/book/*show/52309.The_Autobiography_of_Benjamin_Franklin)

51. John Wooden, *My Personal Best: Life Lessons From an All-American Journey*, (McGraw-Hill Education, 2004)

52. Dr. Bob Rotella, *Make Your Next Shot Your Best Shot*, (Simon & Schuster, New York, NY, 2021)

www.ingramcontent.com/pod-product-compliance
Lightning Source LLC
LaVergne TN
LVHW021804060526
838201LV00058B/3236